CONTENTS

FOREWORD

The Abu Ghraib prison scandal cast a spotlight on the use of contractors to perform functions normally associated with military personnel, and all the contracting, control, discipline, and training issues associated therewith. The sometimes-overheated rhetoric of the press created an impression that the use of contractor personnel to perform functions traditionally considered to be the realm of uniformed personnel was something new and extraordinary. It is neither, though the number of intelligence-related functions performed by contractors during combat operations in Iraq and Afghanistan may, indeed, be unprecedented.

The extensive use of contractor personnel to augment military intelligence operations is now an established fact of life and, occasional contracting "scandals" notwithstanding, any effective and efficient design for intelligence support to operating forces must provide for their use. The civilian sector can respond to rapidly changing requirements of the Global War on Terror with flexibility and speed that the government sector does not possess. And, in a number of cases, the civilian sector possesses technology, equipment, and technological know-how that the government sector could not acquire in any reasonable amount of time. Add to this the problem of end-strength limitations and recruiting and retention problems, and it is apparent that contractors are a permanent part of the intelligence landscape.

But this dependence on contractors comes with its own set of problems, most of which stem from inadequate planning and from lack of training of deployed uniformed personnel in the intricacies of contracting for and administering contractor personnel. The author points out certain steps that must be taken to provide for effective management of contractor personnel in the field, and, indeed, the Army even has a Field Manual devoted to contractor administration which brings out many of the same points (FM 3-100.26, "Contractors on the Battlefield"). Yet uniformed intelligence personnel continue to be deployed without adequate training and preparation to handle contractors who will be supporting them.

The author suggests evaluation standards for the use of contractors and possible long-term initiatives to reduce dependence on traditional "outside" contractors. His suggestions are worthy of serious consideration. But in the meantime, contractors will continue to be a part of the Table of Organization and Equipment (TO&E) of deploying intelligence personnel engaged in counterterrorism operations. We have a responsibility to train our uniformed personnel in the use of contractors just as we would prepare and train them to use any other item on their deploying TO&E.

Thomas A. Brooks
Rear Admiral, U.S. Navy (ret)
Former Director of Naval Intelligence

INTELLIGENCE COMMERCIALIZATION: PRIVATE SECTOR AUGMENTATION FOR OPERATIONAL SUPPORT

The end of the Cold War presented a paradoxical dilemma for the Intelligence Community (IC). The demise of the Soviet Union brought about a significant downsizing of the nation's intelligence apparatus while concurrently necessitating a major reallocation of intelligence resources to cover a more complex array of trans-national threats such as counter-proliferation, terrorism, organized crime, drug trafficking, and ethno-political conflict.[1] The combination of shrinking budgets and expanding analytical requirements placed enormous demands on the Community. Among the most pressing challenges was the need for an on-demand, surged intelligence capability for coverage over a diverse range of operational requirements.

A key recommendation of a 1996 House Permanent Select Committee investigation of the nation's intelligence capabilities called for the creation of a dynamic surge capacity for crisis response. The Committee concluded that such resources "need not be self-contained within the IC," but must be quickly marshaled "without undue concerns about who owns the assets."[2] Several other independent reform studies at the time proposed initiatives to satisfy surged collection demands by leveraging non-governmental resources.[3]

Despite these recommendations, during the 1990s there was little effort to create such a surge capacity. Bureaucratic inertia and lack of clear consensus on an intelligence reform agenda made major initiatives impossible. With the enormous intelligence demands of the Global War on Terrorism (GWOT) the issue of surge capacity has reemerged as a critical issue for community leaders. Collection management, remote sensing, linguistic support, document exploitation, interrogation, and technical analysis are just some intelligence support functions currently being performed by private contractors.

---

[1] Total military end strength from 1989-1999 fell from approximately 2.1 to 1.4 million. U.S. Congress, House Permanent Select Committee on Intelligence, *IC21: Intelligence Community in the 21st Century*, 104th Cong., 1996, chapter 13 "The Cost of Intelligence," URL: <*http://www.gpoaccess.gov/int/int017.html*>, accessed 6 March 2006. Cited hereafter as IC21. Military manpower estimates are cited in Edward Bruner, *Military Forces: What is the Appropriate Size for the United States* (Washington, DC: Congressional Research Service, May 2004), 1.

[2] *IC21*, 10.

[3] Several notable reports from the period proposed various public-private partnerships for IC surge capabilities. Examples include: The Commission on the Roles and Capabilities of the U.S. Intelligence Community, *Preparing for the 21st Century: An Appraisal of U.S. Intelligence* (Washington DC: U.S. Government Printing Office, 1996), xxi, URL: <*http://www.access.gpo.gov/int/report.html*>, accessed 11 August 2004; The Council on Foreign Relations. *Making Intelligence Smarter: The Future of U.S. Intelligence, Report of an Independent Task Force* (1996) 3, URL: <*http://www.copi.com/articles/intelrpt/cfr.html*>, accessed 10 Aug 2004; Allan Goodman and others, *In from the Cold: The Report of the Twentieth Century Fund Task Force on the Future of U.S. Intelligence* (New York: The Twentieth Century Fund Press, 1996), 65.

This ad hoc response to meet the intelligence requirements of GWOT operations has produced mixed results. One report strongly recommended the permanent integration of commercial imagery products into the conventional collection management cycle for operational commanders.[4] Conversely, a key finding of the Army Inspector General's report on OIF detainee operations in Iraq clearly identified poor training and misuse of contract interrogators as a contributing factor in detainee abuse.[5]

These examples speak to both the promise and the liability of utilizing commercial augmentation for intelligence surge capacity. Given the current mismatch between operational requirements and intelligence force structure, there will be continuing reliance on commercial augmentation. As critical intelligence requirements are increasingly resourced through commercial augmentation, IC leaders must determine the appropriate roles for private sector firms and provide effective plans for legal oversight, operational integration, and management of contracted support.

To date, few studies have adequately considered the policy implications of integrating non-governmental providers into the operational intelligence cycle.[6] GWOT operations have required significant reliance on private sector resources for intelligence collection and analysis but have done so without sufficient measures for effective acquisition, management and accountability over commercial providers.

This study assesses the value of current commercial activities used within DoD elements of the Intelligence Community, particularly dealing with operational functions such as analysis, collection management, document exploitation, interrogation, production, and linguistic support. These functions were selected due to the extensive use of commercial augmentation in these areas during recent GWOT operations.

The author conducted data collection and interviewed personnel assigned within DoD agencies, Combined Command, and Joint Task Force intelligence staffs. A holistic evaluation of current contract management practices was conducted using findings from several recent government studies and critiques of ongoing commercialization initiatives. The evaluation focused primarily on the efficacy of the contract development process, management procedures, and how commercial services were integrated into the operational intelligence cycle.

---

[4] Joint Forces Command, "Joint Lessons Learned: Operation IRAQI FREEDOM Major Combat Operations," unpublished coordinating draft report, 1 March 2004.

[5] Department of the Army, Office of the Inspector General, *Detainee Operations Inspection*, 21 July 2004, URL: <*http://www4.army.mil/ocpa/reports/ArmyIGDetaineeAbuse*>, accessed 16 August 2004.

[6] A notable exception is a 2000 monograph that examined the growth of commercialized competitive intelligence and its impact on the government monopoly over sensitive information. This study considered the expanding role of private corporations in the collection, analysis and dissemination of intelligence-related information and how this phenomenon challenges traditional government prerogatives as well as notions of public privacy. James R. Sutton, *Subversion of a Government Monopoly: The Privatization of Intelligence Services* (Erie, PA: Research Intelligence Consortium, Inc, February 2000).

Selected List of Organizational Interviews and Questionnaire Respondents[7]

Army G2	Plans and Operations Linguist/interrogation support
INSCOM	Contracting authority office
SOUTHCOM	JTF-170/JTF Guantanamo
CENTCOM	CJTF-180/CFC Afghanistan CJTF-7/MNF-MNC Iraq
EUCOM	EUCOM, G2 JTF-Eagle (Bosnia-Herzegovina) JTF-Falcon (Kosovo) JAC (Molesworth)

---

[7] Data collection was conducted through face-to-face interviews when possible, otherwise by telephonic interview and written research questionnaires. A complete listing of all organizations and individuals queried for this research is found in Glenn J. Voelz, MAJ, USA, *Managing the Private Spies: The Use of Commercial Augmentation for Intelligence Operations.* MSSI Thesis (Washington, DC: Joint Military Intelligence College, 2005). The thesis bibliography contains a complete list of interviews as well as a sample of the written research questionnaire.

HISTORICAL PRECEDENTS FOR
COMMERCIALIZED INTELLIGENCE

*In all countries engaged in war, experience has sooner or later pointed out that
contracts with private men of substance and understanding are necessary for the
subsistence, covering, clothing, and moving of any Army.[8]*

— Robert Morris, *Superintendent of Finance, 1781*

Despite increased public attention focused on the practice of "outsourcing"
intelligence support functions, this phenomenon is certainly not unprecedented. Indeed,
it was not until the early 20th century that the United States possessed a professionally
trained, organic intelligence capability within the government. Prior to that time
military intelligence was largely an improvised affair, conducted by cavalry scouts
and managed by line officers with no formal intelligence training.[9] Due to the lack of
dedicated personnel, the collection and analysis of intelligence information was often
delegated to civilian auxiliaries employed on short-term assignments for specified
tasks. In many respects, the current system of ad hoc commercial augmentation is
similar to the earliest practices used by the military to satisfy short-term intelligence
needs.

During the American Revolution the absence of a professional intelligence staff
required augmentation by civilian spy networks to supplement military reconnaissance.
It is estimated that General Washington spent more than 10 percent of his wartime
expenditures on intelligence related activities, much of this funding to support civilian
agents collecting critical information on British operations.[10] Among the most notable
examples was Washington's use of the Culper spy ring in British-occupied New York
City. This spy network was managed by officers under Washington's command but
most of the actual collectors were civilian auxiliaries who were paid for services as
required.

Following the war most of the army's intelligence functions were informally
delegated to topographic engineers, signal officers, or cavalry scouts, but throughout

---

[8] Quote reprinted from preface of the U.S. Army, Pamphlet 715-16 (Procurement), *Contractor
Deployment Guide* (27 February 1998), URL: *<http://www.army.mil/usapa/epubs/pdf/p715_16.pdf>*,
accessed 5 November 2004.

[9] The formation of the Division of Military Information in 1885 was the first permanent intelligence
organization established by the U.S. Army. This organization eventually comprised a small staff of foreign
attaches, topographical experts, and engineering and technical specialists. Despite the great demand for
intelligence during the Spanish-American War and WWI, the Military Information Division remained
a backwater assignment on the War Department's General Staff. The establishment of the Military
Intelligence Division during WWII was the first permanent, professionalized organization dedicated to such
matters. A useful account is provided in John Patrick Finnegan, *Army Lineage Series: Military Intelligence*
(Washington, DC: Center of Military History, 1998), URL: *<http://www.army.mil/cmh-pg/books/Lineage/
mi/mi-fm.html>*, accessed 21 October 2004.

[10] P. K. Rose, *The Founding Fathers of American Intelligence* (Washington DC: CIA Center for the Study
of Intelligence, 1999), URL: *<http://www.cia.gov/csi/books/940299/art-1.html>*, accessed 21 October
2004.

the 19th century regular army assets were frequently supplemented by non-military specialists to provide unique skills or expertise. One such example from the Mexican American War was the so-called "Mexican Spy Company," a quasi-military force contracted by American commanders to provide local intelligence, counter-espionage services, surveillance, and route reconnaissance in support of U.S. forces.[11]

When military operations began in Mexico there was virtually no knowledge among American officers of the political intentions of the Mexican government or movements and capabilities of the enemy army. Lieutenant George G. Meade reported that among the 4,000 American troops serving in Northern Mexico at the time, none could speak Spanish.[12] Locally hired augmentation was critical for providing intelligence support to military commanders and for effective counter-intelligence and counter-espionage operations. During U.S. military operations between Veracruz and Mexico City nearly 200 civilian augmentees were drawn from ranks of local bandits and Mexican army deserters. These contract collectors were organized into several operational companies under the direct command of Major General Winfield Scott.[13] During the course of the campaign over $15,000 was distributed by local commanders for the hire of civilian augmentees to satisfy a wide range of intelligence functions and linguistic support.[14]

During the Civil War intelligence support remained mostly a non-specialized discipline. The army's reliance on contracted civilian augmentation remained a common practice, perhaps mostly famously with General George McClellan's use of Allen Pinkerton's detective agency.[15] Pinkerton's agency was a strictly private enterprise but served a quasi-governmental role as one of McClellan's primary intelligence gathering tools for the Union Army. Pinkerton's private agents conducted a wide range of intelligence functions including surveillance operations in the Confederate capital, counter-espionage investigations behind Union lines, exploitation of captured documents and field reports, and interrogations of Confederate prisoners and deserters.

Pinkerton's efforts were supplemented by another intelligence entrepreneur named Lafayette Baker who operated a private company conducting counter-espionage investigations and military police work for the Union army.[16] Baker worked directly for the War Department and focused his efforts primarily on intercepting contraband mail and merchandise moving into Confederate territory, as well as exposing disloyal Union businessmen engaging in illicit trade across enemy lines.

The exploits of these private intelligence services have been romanticized in

---

[11] Finnegan, 8.

[12] Brook A. Caruso, *The Mexican Spy Company: United States Covert Operations in Mexico, 1845-1848* (Jefferson, NC: McFarland and Company Inc., 1991), 84.

[13] Caruso, 153.

[14] Caruso, 157.

[15] Perhaps the single best monograph on intelligence during the Civil War is Edwin C. Fishel, *The Secret War for the Union: The Untold Story of Military Intelligence in the Civil War* (Boston: Houghton Mifflin, 1996). This text provides an exhaustive description of the war's intelligence operations, both commercial and governmental.

[16] Fishel, 55.

popular history though their actual contribution to the Union effort remains somewhat questionable.[17] Pinkerton's erroneous intelligence reports are suspected of contributing to General McClellan's overestimation of Confederate forces during his timid peninsular campaign of 1862. Furthermore, these contract spies were generally weak at collecting timely and accurate intelligence on Confederate military intentions although they did enjoy limited success with counter-intelligence and counter-espionage operations.

In the post-Civil War era the Pinkerton Detective Agency expanded its operations to become a prototype for modern corporate intelligence and security, providing protective and investigative service for industry, railroads, and local law enforcement. Pinkerton's men revolutionized the use of "mug shots" and developed an extensive criminal database used by local law enforcement organizations. The agency also performed operational functions such as surveillance, as well as several high profile "manhunts" like the legendary pursuit of Butch Cassidy and the "Sundance Kid."

Despite these successes, the agency's activities attracted significant public scrutiny after a violent confrontation in 1892 with striking workers at the Carnegie Steel Mill in Homestead, Pennsylvania. In the aftermath of the bloody tragedy, public outcry by labor organizations led Congress to enact a law restricting government contracting with "Pinkerton Detective Agencies or similar organizations."[18] This statute remains a part of the Federal Acquisition Regulation to this day and prohibits the government contracting with "quasi-military armed forces."[19]

Despite the mixed results from the employment of commercial intelligence augmentation, the practice continued throughout the remainder of the 19th century. During the army's frontier operations, military commanders frequently employed civilian scouts, interpreters, and local informants when operating in unknown territory. These individuals provided military commanders with a base of local experience, as well as specialized linguistic and cultural knowledge that was invaluable for frontier

---

[17] Fishel, 100.

[18] 5 U.S.C. § 3108 (Employment of detective agencies; restrictions). Also see the Federal Acquisition Regulation (FAR) 37.109 Services of Quasi-Military Armed Forces: "Contracts with Pinkerton Detective Agencies or similar organizations are prohibited by 5 U.S.C. 3108. This prohibition applies only to contracts with organizations that offer quasi-military armed forces for hire, or with their employees, regardless of the contract's character. An organization providing guard or protective services does not thereby become a quasi-military armed force, even though the guards are armed or the organization provides general investigative or detective services."

[19] FAR, Chapter 37.109. The "Anti-Pinkerton Act" resurfaced again in a 1977 case Weinberger v. Equifax, Inc., challenging the government's use of a private corporation for data collection on individual citizens. In this case, the plaintiff argued that Equifax used "detective-like investigative techniques" on behalf of the government. Although the court ruled that the defendant's actions were not illegal, it failed to clarify what actions or characteristics might constitute a "quasi-military armed force." Given the courts' narrow interpretation of the Pinkerton Act, the statute has not yet resurfaced to challenge any of the government's recent contracting for intelligence-related services. Under existing legal interpretations the FAR restriction has not placed a significant limitation on the government's authority to contract for intelligence related services. Additional legal issues concerning intelligence contracting are discussed in Chapter 3. For additional information on the legislative history and interpretations of the Pinkerton Act, see MAJ Gregory L. Bowman, USA, "Transforming Installation Security: Where Do We Go from Here," Military Law Review 178 (Winter 2003), 50-93.

constabulary duties. Perhaps the most famous of these freelance scouts was Buffalo Bill Cody, who served on several occasions as an advisor to military commanders in the West.[20] These short-term, contract scouts were assigned under the Quartermaster Department and generally classified as "laborers," without any formal rank or position of direct authority over troops.[21]

In 1866 Congress formally authorized the hiring of Native American augmentees for scouting and intelligence related services. The Indian scouts primarily conducted reconnaissance operations, "locating the enemy and determining his strength, determining the tribal affiliations of unknown Indians, and all other duties connected with Military Intelligence."[22] Indian scouts were not considered regular enlistees but were hired at the discretion of local commanders for short-term operational needs. The rationale for this approach was economical as well as tactical. In his work on the Indian scouts, historian Thomas Dunlay noted that, after the post-Civil War demobilization, "the employment of Indian scouts may have seemed an economical measure, since it would increase the effectiveness of the small regular force, and Indian enlistments could be terminated in case of need, unlike the fixed five-year enlistments of white and black soldiers."[23]

Much like modern contractors, the Indian scouts were not organized into the Army's regimental system and were generally used only for short periods of duty based upon operational needs. The statute governing their employment stipulated that "they shall be discharged when the necessity for their service shall cease, or at the discretion of the department commander."[24] Acknowledging their irregular status, Congress established that the temporary scouts would "furnish their own horses and horse-equipment, [and] shall be entitled to forty cents per day for their use and risk so long as thus employed."[25]

The Indian scouts provided intelligence, reconnaissance, and translation services supporting frontier campaigns into the 1890s and were used again during the army's Punitive Expedition against Mexico in 1916.[26] The policies for short-term contracting of Indian scouts were modified somewhat during the First World War, with the legislation revised to enlist Indian scouts for 7-year tours like other army soldiers, thus ending their irregular status.

---

[20] Finnegan, 3.

[21] Thomas E. Dowling, *Intelligence in the Final Indian Wars, 1866-1887*, MSSI Thesis (Washington, DC: Joint Military Intelligence College, 1996), 135.

[22] Thomas W. Dunlay, *Wolves for the Blue Soldiers: Indian Scouts and Auxiliaries with the United States Army*, 1860-90 (Lincoln: University of Nebraska Press), 1982, 8.

[23] Dunlay, 44.

[24] U.S. Congress, *Permanent General Laws Relating to Indian Affairs, Revised Statues*, 44th Cong., 1st sess., 1876, Title XIV, Chapter 3, Sec. 1112 Indian Scouts. URL: <http://digital.library.okstate.edu/kappler/Vol1/HTML_files/p1_22img.html>, accessed 29 October 2004.

[25] *Permanent General Laws Relating to Indian Affairs.*

[26] James P. Finley, "Apache Scouts in the Punitive Expedition," *Huachuca Illustrated* 1, 1993, 3, URL: *<http://www.lib.byu.edu/~rdh/wwi/comment/huachuca/HI1-23.htm>*, accessed 28 October 2004.

> ## The Indian Wars — The Rest of the Story [27]
>
> Thomas Dowling's *Intelligence in the Final Indian Wars, 1866-1887*
> addresses the U.S. government's ability to hire Indian Scouts and how
> this was done.
>
> Dowling's research focused on intelligence during the Final Indian
> Wars, and in one chapter gives an interesting accounting of the
> Army's challenge in the hiring of Indian Scouts and other contract
> employees. Unlike the British and French in their colonial empires,
> where they hired native troops and formed them into units, the
> Americans hired the Indians only for selected campaigns, and
> for six months at a time. Dowling explains the reasons for the
> differences.

During this same period, Arthur L. Wagner, an officer with extensive service on the
western frontier, wrote one of the army's first doctrinal works on military intelligence.
Wagner made special note of the utility of temporary augmentation, specifically citing
the use of private spies and Indian scouts as invaluable tools for intelligence gathering.
Despite the advantages of using non-governmental augmentation, Wagner made
particular mention of the liabilities of employing those motivated by profit rather than
"driven by patriotism or a sense of military duty."[28] Based upon his experience, Wagner
cautioned that "the services of a spy permanently attached to a command are likely to be
much more valuable than those of one who is employed only for the single occasion, and
whose efforts are not stimulated by a hope of profitable employment in the future."[29]

By the beginning of the 20th century, several factors lessened the army's reliance on
non-governmental augmentation for intelligence-related tasks. Following the Spanish-
American War the military's new expeditionary orientation awakened leaders to the
necessity of a permanent and specialized corps of intelligence officers. As a result of
this new strategic focus the War Department and Army General Staff finally developed
a permanent, organic intelligence staff section.[30] This change led to an expansion of the
army's foreign attaché program and the creation of the Military Information Division.

This movement toward greater professionalization of intelligence continued through
World War Two and rapidly expanded during the Cold War era. By the post-war period
intelligence had become primarily a governmental affair, dominated by trained experts,
managed by guarded bureaucracies, and highly dependent upon technical collection
capabilities. Large Cold War intelligence budgets and a narrowly defined collection focus
on the Soviet Union fed the growth of an expansive federal infrastructure to support the

---

[27] Dowling, *Intelligence in the Final Indian Wars.*

[28] Arthur L. Wagner, *The Service of Security and Information* (Washington, DC: James L. Chapman, 1893), 200.

[29] Wagner, 202.

[30] Finnegan, 6.

nation's intelligence needs. This state-centered approach to Cold War intelligence found little use for the short-term employment of private wayfarers or commercial, human-intelligence entrepreneurs.

This government-centric approach to intelligence persisted until the mid-1990s when several factors fueled the reentry of commercial providers into fields previously reserved for military and permanent civil service employees. The first event was the dramatic shift of intelligence emphasis away the Soviet Union following the end of the Cold War. The 1990s brought about a broad diversification of national security concerns with a rapid succession of contingency operations falling outside the traditional areas of intelligence focus. Supporting such diverse operational tasks, particularly for intelligence functions such as translation, debriefing, and document exploitation in target languages where the military did not maintain sufficient levels of trained personnel, presented challenges. The use of private sector linguist support was critical for operations in Somalia, Haiti, Bosnia, and Kosovo.[31] This only increased in the wake of 9/11. At present there are over 6,000 private contract linguists supporting various operations in the Global War on Terrorism at a total annual cost exceeding $250 million.[32]

A second major catalyst was the Clinton administration's 1994 National Performance Review (NPR), an initiative intended to "radically change the way government operates—to shift from top down bureaucracy to entrepreneurial government."[33] The Clinton reform agenda emphasized competition, privatization, and commercial outsourcing as methods for improving public sector efficiency and performance. Congress actively supported this process through a broad liberalization of the Federal Acquisition Regulation, the streamlining of contracting procedures, and legislation designed to promote market-based management strategies in governance.[34]

---

[31] During the two-year U.S. involvement in Somalia many contract linguists were employed at the high point of ground operations, at a cost of $8 million. Over 100 contract linguists were used during operations in Haiti, at a cost of $4.6 million. In FY99, over 450 linguists supported operations in Bosnia, while over 430 were employed in Kosovo at an annual cost of $36 million. Of these contract linguists, only U.S. citizens with current security clearances were used for intelligence-related functions. Department of the Army, Office of the Deputy Chief of Staff for Intelligence, *Army Language Master Plan*, 3 January 2000, 75.

[32] This number includes all three categories of contract linguists. AT 1: local national hires with security screening but no clearance. CAT 2: U.S. citizen hires with Secret level clearance. CAT 3: U.S. citizen hires with TS/SCI clearance. Only CAT 2 and CAT 3 hires are permitted to work on sensitive intelligence functions. Lynn McCann, Army Language Support Contracting Officer, Army G2, Intelligence Plans and Operations Directorate, interview by the author, 22 October 2004. Budget figures for GWOT contract language operations are cited in LTG Keith B. Alexander, USA, Army Deputy Chief of Staff for Intelligence (Army G-2), Statement before the Committee on Armed Services Subcommittee on Strategic Forces. 108th Cong., 2d sess., 7 April 2004. URL: <*http://armed-services.senate.gov/statemnt/2004/April/Alexander.pdf*>, accessed 2 May 2005.

[33] A useful overview of the NPR and its implications is provided in George Nestercznk, "Reviewing the National Performance Review," *Regulation* 19, no. 3 (1996), URL: <*http://www.cato.org/pubs/regulation/reg19n3b.html*>, accessed 10 November 2004.

[34] Most notable among these initiatives was the 1994 Federal Acquisitions Streamlining Act. This legislation eliminated or revised hundreds of statutes dealing with government acquisition and contracting. These changes were complemented by the 1996 Federal Acquisition Reform Act (Clinger-Cohen Act). Together, these reforms dramatically transformed the government's relationship with the private sector and encouraged a wide variety of public-private partnerships for product and service acquisition.

Concurrent with the Clinton administration's NPR initiative was a significant post-Cold War military downsizing and large reductions in Department of Defense intelligence personnel. Between 1992 and 1996, the Department of Defense experienced a 16 percent decrease in total personnel, with DoD reductions representing 75 percent of the overall federal government drawdown during the period.[35] As a result, nearly all of the agencies within the Intelligence Community experienced sharp personnel declines throughout the decade.[36]

With significant reductions in personnel authorizations, combined with the goal of "reinventing government" through entrepreneurial initiatives, DoD and other agencies aggressively sought to "outsource" many support functions to private sector providers. Initially, much of the commercial augmentation established after the NPR was aimed at administrative functions, clerical work, basic maintenance, and labor services. However, privatization efforts soon widened to include highly technical functions such as budgetary analysis, procurement, personnel services, and logistics.

This trend toward greater reliance on market-based management strategies continues today. The most recent guidance provided in the Quadrennial Defense Review states that "only those functions that must be performed by DoD should be kept by DoD. Any function that can be provided by the private sector is not a core government function."[37] The Bush administration has continued aggressive commercialization initiatives and actively pursued opportunities to privatize many DoD functions traditionally performed by military and civil service personnel. Consistent with this overall trend, in recent years DoD intelligence organizations have greatly expanded use of commercial resources to augment a wide range of operational requirements.

JUSTIFYING INTELLIGENCE OUTSOURCING

By some accounts the logistical support, security, and intelligence-related functions have essentially become an "organic" element of combat power. Indeed, over the past decade the growth of commercial support to military operations has been dramatic. The market for privatized military support is now nearly half of the Department of Defense total annual expenditures.[38] Equally dramatic has been the major shift in Pentagon acquisition away from product procurement toward services contracting. In the mid-1980s approximately two-thirds of the Pentagon's contracting budget went for the purchase of goods and infrastructure. Today, over half of all DoD contract dollars

---

[35] Nestercznk. Table 2. Source: OPM Employment Trend reports and the OMB budget documents.

[36] Personnel levels for NSA, DIA, and CIA declined throughout the 1990s. The single exception was a small increase in DIA personnel levels in 1992 and 1996 due to an inter-governmental transfer of functions. Actual personnel numbers are classified but percentage changes are available in *Preparing for the 21st Century: An Appraisal of U.S. Intelligence*, Figure 9-2, "Cumulative Change in Civilian Personnel Since 1980."

[37] U.S. Department of Defense, *Quadrennial Defense Review: America's Security in the 21st Century* (Washington, DC: Government Printing Office), 2001, 53.

[38] Mahlon Apgar and John Keane, "New Business with the New Military," *Harvard Business Review,* (September 2004), 45.

are used to acquire services.[39] This figure represents a 90 percent increase in service contracting since 1993.[40]

According to a Government Accountability Office (GAO) report, overall spending on service contracts with military support providers amounted to $118 billion in 2003.[41] It is estimated that nearly half of the entire 2004 U.S. intelligence budget was spent on the procurement of commercial systems and operational support services.[42]

Although greatly expanded in recent years, this trend toward increasing privatization of intelligence support predates GWOT operations. Throughout the 1990s private sector intelligence and security firms provided significant support to the Pentagon in the war on drugs in Colombia and for surveillance activities along the U.S. border.[43] More recently, the Army's Intelligence and Security Command (INSCOM) announced a new $209 million contract for intelligence support services including information technology and force management, administrative support, and "intelligence, security, and information operations." This contract provides support for a wide range of intelligence operations in DoD's major regional commands.[44] Given recent trends, commercial augmentation for intelligence functions is likely to remain a significant, if not expanding, element of the nation's operational capability.

There are three primary reasons for the government's expanding dependence upon private sector resources for intelligence augmentation. First, commercial augmentation has been used primarily as an ad hoc measure to mitigate critical intelligence

---

[39] Larry Makinson, "Outsourcing the Pentagon," Center for Public Integrity, 29 September 2004, URL: <http://www.publicintegrity.org/pns/>, accessed 30 September 2004.

[40] Mary H. Cooper, "Privatizing the Military," *CQ Researcher* 14, No. 24, 25 (June 2004), 568. From 1992-1999, DoD expenditures on service procurement increased from $39.9 billion to $51.8 billion. For the first time in 1999, the total dollars spent on services equaled the amount spent on goods and infrastructure. This trend has only increased since 2001 with the enormous manpower and service support needs associated with the Global War on Terrorism. J. S. Gansler, Under Secretary of Defense for Acquisition and Technology, "Guidebook for Performance-Based Services Acquisition (PBSA) in the Department of Defense," 2 January 2001, URL: <http://www.acq.osd.mil/dpap/Docs/pbsaguide010201.pdf>, accessed 2 May 2005.

[41] Government Accountability Office, *Contract Management: Opportunities to Improve Surveillance on the Department of Defense Service Contracts,* Report Abstract, Contract GAO-05-274, March 17, 2005 URL: <http:www.gao.gov/docdblite/summary.php?rptno=GAO-05-274&accno=A19596>, accessed 7 March 2006.

[42] This figure marked a significant increase from pre-9/11 estimates of approximately $71 billion. Michael J. Grinfeld, "War Incorporated," *California Lawyer* (May 2005), 24. Estimate for the 2004 budget from Tim Shorrock, "The Spy who Billed Me," *Mother Jones* (January-February 2005), URL: <http://www.motherjones.com/news/outfront/2005/01/12_400.html>, accessed 8 March 2005.

[43] *Fortune* reported several companies under contract with DoD and the State Department for surveillance and intelligence-related activities in support of counter-drug operations in Colombia. Contractors included Airscan, Northrop Grumman and DynCorp. Nelson D. Schwartz and Noshua Watson, "The Pentagon's Private Army," *Fortune*, 17 March 2003, 101.

[44] The INSCOM contract includes a team led by ManTech International, L-3 Communications Corp, SAIC, and Systex. The companies will provide intelligence support services for Pacific Command, European Command, Central Command, Southern Command, U.S. Forces Korea, and Northern Command. Tim Starks, "ManTech Wins a Seat on Defense Intelligence and Security Contract," *CQ.com Homeland Security*, 25 January 2005, URL: <http://www.cqhls.com/hs/display.do?dockey/cqonline/prod/data/docs/html>, accessed 17 March 2005.

manpower shortages resulting from post-Cold War force structure reductions. Second, the increasing complexity of the threat environment has required a rapid recalibration of collection and analytical capabilities to acquire unique skill-sets currently underrepresented within the intelligence civil service. Third, the informational tools needed to combat trans-national terrorism have required exploitation of non-traditional intelligence methodologies and an increasing dependence on commercial technology and analytical systems. The following section addresses each of these issues in detail.

Overcoming Force Structure Challenges

The most fundamental reason for using contract support during recent contingency operations has been to mitigate acute shortages of military and civil service intelligence personnel. Since the beginning of GWOT operations there have been numerous reports of personnel shortfalls among forward-deployed intelligence organizations. These manpower shortages have had a detrimental impact on the collection and analytical capability of intelligence organizations.

A major after-action review of Operation ENDURING FREEDOM (OEF) found that the "demands on intelligence were never greater. Limitations on the number of personnel restricted the ability of organizations to analyze information and develop products using the processes and tools practiced in our training centers."[45] These intelligence manning shortfalls in Afghanistan "considerably raised the risk to operations...by forcing intelligence staff to operate on the margin between success and failure." Early in OEF, the intelligence Analysis and Control Element for the coalition forces command "functioned at less that 30 percent strength." [46] In particular, military leaders cited significant shortfalls in high-demand intelligence skills such as analysts, interrogators, and linguistic support. Commercial contracting was the only method available to acquire the needed manpower for support to these military operations.

---

[45] U.S. Army Central Command, Combined Arms Assessment Team, "OPERATION ENDURING FREEDOM: CAAT Initial Impressions Report," (Leavenworth: Center for Army Lessons Learned, 2002), 44, URL: <*https://www.//call2.army.mil/products/iir/asp/BOSNIA/BHCAAT2/html/appc.asp*>, accessed 3 September 2004.

[46] "OPERATION ENDURING FREEDOM: CAAT Initial Impressions Report," 45.

Private Military Companies — What Role Do They Play?[47]

In his *Peacekeeping for Hire? The Potential Role of Private Military Companies in Peace Operations,* Scott Strohecker discusses whether private military companies (PMCs) are upscale mercenaries or the latest step in outsourcing, and whether they can be effective as peacekeepers.

Strohecker wrote prior to American involvement in Afghanistan and Iraq, and his focus was particularly on the use of private armies and mercenaries in Africa and in the Balkans. Sometimes the line separating mercenary from military has been tenuous. In the Balkans the Americans supported contractors, often retired military, working for the U.S. Government to train the new militaries as new nations split off from the former Yugoslavia, and internal strife spread. In Africa, private concerns were hired by beleaguered governments to shore up their fragile control. Some of these mercenaries were considered thugs, and some were considered military professionals, hiring themselves out much as the contractors were in the Balkans.

This study evaluates PMCs to determine their potential effectiveness in a peacekeeping role. Three industry leaders are examined: Executive Outcomes (EO) of South Africa, Sandline International of Britain, and Military Professional Resources Inc. (MPRI) from the United States. Study results indicate that although PMCs maintain several unique and useful capabilities, their role in peacekeeping/peace enforcement operations will be limited.

Such manpower problems were not limited to the Afghanistan campaign. The after-action review for 3rd Infantry Division during the initial stages of Operation IRAQI FREEDOM (OIF) noted critical shortages of intelligence personnel, observing that units "did not have sufficient capability to man an enemy prisoner of war cage, to surge collection, or conduct general support operations, or provide experienced and comprehensive analysis and guidance to operational teams."[48] These manpower shortages caused significant delays in the tactical screening and interrogation of detainees during the early stages of the occupation. A separate OEF study group similarly observed that the "demand for linguists (interrogators, interpreters, voice intercepts, document exploiters) continues to significantly exceeded [sic] supply."[49] Additionally, investigations of the Abu Ghraib abuse incidents made specific mention of acute shortages of personnel trained for human intelligence collection and analysis,

---

[47] Scott Strohecker, *Peacekeeping for Hire? The Potential Role of Private Military Companies in Peace Operations*, unpublished MSSI Thesis, Washington, DC: Joint Military Intelligence College, 1999.

[48] U.S. Army Third Infantry Division, "OPERATION IRAQI FREEDOM Lessons Learned," May 2003, Leavenworth: Center for Army Lessons Learned, URL: *<https://www.//call2.army.mil/products/on-point/ asp/>*, accessed 14 November 2004.

[49] OPERATION IRAQI FREEDOM Study Group, Intelligence Battlefield Operating System Initial Observations, (Leavenworth: Center for Army Lessons Learned, 19 June 2003), URL: *<https://www.//call2. army.mil/products/on-point/asp/>*, accessed 13 November 2004.

noting that the "lack of manning provided significant challenges due to the increased mission work load and the environment."[50]

Outside of the OEF and OIF theaters, soon after detainees began arriving at the Joint Detention Facility in Guantanamo Bay, several contracts were awarded to supplement intelligence operations, including linguist support, interrogation, document exploitation, and analytical functions. An on-site linguist contract manager observed that, "the military just did not have enough personnel and couldn't keep them there long enough to take advantage of their experience, so contractors had to be hired to supplement the shortages."[51]

Although GWOT operations have exacerbated intelligence personnel shortfalls, even routine, non-contingency operations have made extensive use of contract support in recent years. A 2003 General Accounting Office report on DoD management procedures evaluated the use of contractors for analytical and linguistic support to intelligence operations in the Balkans and found that missions such as "Task Force Eagle in Bosnia relies on contracted linguistic and intelligence analyst services... [and] if the contracted services were lost, it would mean an immediate critical loss would occur for the military because DoD does not have service personnel with these skills."[52] A U.S. Army Europe Contracting Officer Representative concurred with this finding, stating that "for watch jobs and other tactical-MI type jobs, we just don't have the soldiers we need to fill all the vacancies and had to contract the positions out."[53]

While DoD has used commercial contracting primarily to mitigate critical personnel shortages, there are other considerations that make private sector augmentation operationally advantageous in certain circumstances. One issue is the challenge of active duty "force caps" in some operational environments. In the Balkans for example, NATO-imposed force structure limitations required that DoD supplement active duty forces with significant numbers of civilian contract personnel to avoid host country legal restrictions on external military forces. Generally speaking, contract personnel do not count against the force structure caps imposed against active duty soldiers.[54] The use of commercial contracting has enabled DoD to effectively "outsource" certain lower priority intelligence missions such as the Balkans while reserving the active duty force for more pressing contingency operations.

---

[50] MG George R. Fay, USA., AR 15-6 *Investigation of the Abu Ghraib Detention Facility and 205th Military Intelligence Brigade*, 2004, 21, URL: <*http://www.globalsecurity.org/intell/library/reports/2004/800-mp-bde.htm*>, accessed 2 May 2005.

[51] All general conclusions drawn from analysis of questionnaire responses will be hereafter cited as Operational Questionnaire. Identification of individual respondents is cited as necessary. The names of some questionnaire respondents have been withheld upon request. A sample of the operational questionnaire can be found in the appendix from Voelz, *Managing the Private Spies*.

[52] Government Accountability Office, *Military Operations: Contractors Provide Vital Services to Deployed Forces but are Not Adequately Addressed in DOD Plans*, GAO-03-695 (June 2003), 18, URL: <*http://www.gao.gov/highlights/d03695high.pdf*>, accessed 13 October 2004.

[53] This comment was provided for non-attribution by an army officer who served for two years as a Contracting Officer Representative for the U.S. Army Europe G2. Operational questionnaire conducted by author, November 2004.

[54] Michael J. Grinfeld, "War Incorporated," *California Lawyer* (May 2005), 25.

The majority of respondents for this study indicated that their organizations used contractor support primarily to supplement shortages of government personnel rather than to augment for non-organic skills.[55] In most cases contract personnel performed similar intelligence functions as their uniformed and civil service counterparts. This fact makes intelligence contracting unique as compared to other types of military outsourcing. Over the past decade much of the commercial privatization of logistical, transportation, and support functions was intended to entirely divest the active force structure of certain sustainment activities. Rather than serving as a supplement to active force capability, support contractors have fully taken over functions considered non-core war-fighting tasks such as meal preparation, laundry services, and routine logistics. Conversely, most intelligence-related contracting has been used to mitigate personnel shortfalls in core-skill area tasks, including some of the most mission-critical collection and analytical functions.

Dealing with a Complex Threat Environment

A second factor encouraging the use of commercial augmentation has been the urgent demand for highly-specialized skills for collection and analysis against unconventional threats in peripheral regions. The dilemma of managing intelligence assets for a diverse and unpredictable range of contingencies has been a subject of concern for some time. The 2001 Quadrennial Defense Review articulated this challenge, noting that "the United States cannot predict with a high degree of confidence the identity of the countries or the actors that may threaten its interests or security."[56] Emerging threat scenarios of the past decade have extended far beyond the traditional intelligence focus on state-based conflict and now encompass a diverse range of issues such as terrorism, weapons proliferation, trans-national crime, piracy, genocide, ethnic conflict, environmental and resource disputes, and threats from pandemic disease and bio-warfare. As one intelligence community reform advocate explained, "in the age of constant surprise and impossible-to-anticipate mutations of the threat, no bureaucracy can be effective."[57]

An important advantage of commercial augmentation is that it can provide bureaucratic organizations with the flexibility to rapidly transform static organic capabilities by providing unique skills-sets for unanticipated requirements. Intelligence reform advocates Bruce Berkowitz and Allan Goodman have suggested that such market-based approaches are a preferred solution for satisfying unpredictable operational needs, noting that

> The intelligence community needs at least as much flexibility as private corporations. Many of its requirements for specialized information are likely to change quickly. Traditional civil service tenure is probably suited only for employees with the most general, long-term skills....Intelligence organizations still need to be able to "surge" and add additional personnel on short-notice, but now the requirement has changed greatly. Today,

---

[55] *Operational Questionnaire.*

[56] *Quadrennial Defense Review: America's Security in the 21st Century,* 3.

[57] Robert David Steele, *The New Craft of Intelligence: Personal, Public and Political* (Oakton, Virginia: OSS International Press, 2002), 155, URL: <*http://www.oss.net/dynamaster/file_archive/020731/ 7e44d06d4268c8b030d47d58c01fca03/chapter15.doc*>, accessed 8 August 2004.

surge capacity is needed not just to add more people with the same skills to handle a greater volume of work, but to find and add people with different skills to meet rapidly changing requirements for analysis.[58]

Berkowitz and Goodman suggest that a modernized intelligence personnel system must have capability to rapidly augment permanent staff with outside expertise that can be bought "by the pound" to help satisfy specific, short-term requirements.

Several intelligence reform studies during the 1990s also urged the development of personnel management systems designed for rapid, ad hoc integration of non-governmental resources for response to unanticipated crises. The 1996 Council on Foreign Relations task force on intelligence reform noted that "analysis would be improved by increasing the flow of talented people into the intelligence community from outside the government."[59] Such programs would provide a flexible resource of non-governmental professional, academic, and subject-matter experts who could provide threat-focused expertise for short-term need. A key finding of the 1996 Aspin-Brown commission on intelligence reform called for a greater use of "substantive experts outside the Intelligence Community" as a tool for improving the quality of analytical products.[60]

To implement such a strategy, Robert David Steele, a noted open-source intelligence advocate, has called for the creation of a network of "intelligence minutemen" from outside the government bureaucracy — individuals mobilized for work on short-term intelligence projects or in response to unique operational requirements. To obtain the best tools for intelligence analysis, Steele suggests that "the center of gravity for both national security and national prosperity lie now in the private sector and its intellectual property."[61]

In recent years, commercial contracting has been the primary tool by which intelligence organizations have developed this ad hoc adaptation capability to quickly leverage specific skills or expertise. The clearest articulation of this approach appears in the Army Language Master Plan, which explicitly states that "training resources do not permit preparing military staff for a wide variety of unknown and hard-to-forecast small-scale conflicts. With limited resources ... the balance of the Army's small-scale conflict needs could be met with contract translators and interpreters."[62] In the GWOT, short-term contracting has clearly become the primary mechanism by which intelligence organizations have built strategic flexibility for unforeseen collection and analytical requirements.

---

[58] Bruce Berkowitz and Allan Goodman, *Best Truth: Intelligence in the Information Age* (New Haven: Yale University Press, 2000), 56.

[59] *Making Intelligence Smarter,* 3.

[60] *Preparing for the 21st Century: An Appraisal of U.S. Intelligence,* xxi.

[61] Robert David Steele, *The New Craft of Intelligence: Personal, Public and Political* (Oakton, Virginia: OSS International Press, 2002), 155, URL: <*http://www.oss.net/dynamaster/file_archive/020731/ 7e44d06d4268c8b030d47d58c01fca03/chapter15.doc*>, accessed 8 August 2004.

[62] Government Accountability Office, *Foreign Languages: Human Capital Approach Needed to Correct Staffing and Proficiency Shortfalls,* GAO-02-375 (January 2002), URL: <*http://www.gao.gov/new.items/ d02375.pdf*>, accessed 13 October 2004.

Commercial augmentation has permitted intelligence organizations to rapidly recalibrate their human capital base to meet changing analytical demands. Whereas the traditional Cold-War era intelligence bureaucracy focused primarily on technical collection and order of battle analysis, counter-insurgency operations in Iraq and Afghanistan have placed a premium on human intelligence, counter-intelligence, interrogation, and language specialists. But a 2002 GAO report on government foreign language resources noted significant shortfalls in Army linguists qualified as translators, interpreters, cryptologic specialists, and human intelligence collectors.[63] The Intelligence Community has been critically short of these "cultural intelligence" skill-sets since the beginning of GWOT operations. The U.S. Army Central Command after-action review of OEF operations noted that "unconventional, distributed warfare placed higher than normal demand on Human Intelligence, which is not resourced at the tactical level."[64] The report found that "the mission of screening and interrogating large numbers of important detainees demanded native-proficiency-level linguists in order to perceive cultural nuance, understand a variety of dialects, and accurately understand acquired information. The most effective means of acquiring native linguists was through contracting."[65]

Shortages of these critical-skill personnel have introduced significant operational risk for U.S. operations in the GWOT. A recent Army investigation of operations at Abu Ghraib noted that "as commanders at all levels sought operational intelligence, it became apparent that the intelligence structure was undermanned, under-equipped, and inappropriately organized for counter-insurgency operations....Technical intelligence collection means alone were insufficient in providing the requisite information on an enemy that had adapted to the environment and to a high-tech opponent."[66]

The rigidity of the Cold War era force structure has created a bureaucracy ill-equipped to rapidly adapt to changing intelligence requirements. As Steele suggests, "intelligence community leadership is going to have to come to grips with the reality that most of the experts are going to be in the private sector and only available 'by the task' rather than as full-time employees."[67] Until the intelligence bureaucracy is reformed to permit more flexible market-based management, the ad hoc use of contract support will continue to be the primary mechanism for acquiring short-term augmentation of highly needed skills.

Integrating Advanced Technical and Analytical Tools

A less-mentioned but increasingly important factor encouraging the use of non-governmental augmentation is the fact of disproportionately rapid advances in

---

[63] GAO, *Foreign Languages.*

[64] "OPERATION ENDURING FREEDOM: CAAT Initial Impressions Report," 56.

[65] "OPERATION ENDURING FREEDOM: CAAT Initial Impressions Report," 55.

[66] U.S. Department of the Army, Office of the Inspector General, *AR 15-6 Investigation of the Abu Ghraib Detention Facility and 205th Military Intelligence Brigade* (2004), 11, URL: <*http://www.globalsecurity. org/intell/library/reports/2004/800-mp-bde.htm*>, accessed 2 May 2005.

[67] *The New Craft of Intelligence: Personal, Public and Political,* 161.

commercial sector processing tools and analytical technology. A basic presumption of Cold War era intelligence was that government held a substantial edge in research and development of advanced collection and analytical systems. But over the past decade this advantage has largely eroded and — according to some — entirely vanished. This disparity is particularly true for high-end technical services such as communications networks, processing tools, automated population of databases, and distributed web-based dissemination — all areas where the private sector has considerably more capability than the legacy systems currently used by most intelligence organizations. As Berkowitz and Goodman have noted in their study on intelligence reform, "the commercial sector will frequently have technology superior to that of government-bound intelligence organizations, and it will almost always be better in developing products and services, and delivering them quickly to users. In some cases, the commercial sector will also have better information."[68]

Several recent examples demonstrate the extent to which private corporations have acquired advanced analytical tools that now exceed the capability of government systems. ChoicePoint Inc. is one such innovator in the field of data processing and analysis that has found considerable work supporting government intelligence and security operations. As company vice president James A. Zimbardi explained, "we do act as an intelligence agency, gathering data, applying analytics."[69] Generally, the private sector is far ahead of government in developing tools for parsing open-source records, conducting automated database population, using identity verification and advanced biometrics tools, computational linguistics and translation, and data-based mapping techniques. Additionally, companies such as LexisNexis Group have found a niche in providing powerful public records processing technology to assist in the analysis of voluminous amounts of non-classified data.[70]

Steele also notes that in recent years the Intelligence Community has generally "failed to keep up with private sector advances in data visualization and organizational memory systems or in advances in collaborative work tools, information communication, and automated monitoring of online and internal information."[71] In order to maintain the most up-to-date technology, the government must essentially become a "customer" of private sector providers. But generally, intelligence organizations have been slow to exploit the best commercial technologies. With the exception of quasi-governmental organizations such as In-Q-Tel, the community

---

[68] *Best Truth: Intelligence in the Information Age*, 23.

[69] Robert O'Harrow, "In Age of Security, Firm Mines Wealth of Personal Data," *Washington Post*, online ed., 20 January 2005, 1, URL: <*http://www.washingtonpost.com/wp-dyn/articles/A22269-2005Jan19.html*>, accessed 20 January 2005.

[70] Both ChoicePoint and LexisNexis Group have negotiated government contracts with U.S. intelligence organizations for data management work. It should be noted that both companies have also recently experienced high-profile security breaches of their corporate databases. Concern over data security is a major unresolved issue that must be addressed as the government pursues public-private partnerships for intelligence. Certainly there are numerous, legitimate counterintelligence concerns as government relies more and more on private sector collection and analytical tools.

[71] Robert David Steele, "Relevant Information: A New Approach to Collection, Sharing and Analysis," Unpublished white paper by the OSS Academy, 15 March 1999, 11. URL: <*http://downloads.securityfocus.com/library/infowar/papers/ISDoctrine.doc*>, accessed 11 May 2005.

has not aggressively sought the integration of commercial off-the-shelf technologies into its collection and analysis capabilities.[72]

Given current trends, it is unlikely that governmental intelligence organizations will ever regain a monopoly on the development of the most advanced technical tools, but Steele suggests that these resources may be exploited by developing "a process for leveraging private sector commercial fee-for-service offerings."[73] In fact, many commercialization advocates assert that certain "open source" functions may be better performed by the private sector than by government agencies. This might include such functions as wide-area surveillance, remote sensing, foreign broadcast transcription and translation, document exploitation, and Internet database exploitation. In many cases the technological capabilities and organizational structure of private sector providers are far better suited for performing these highly technical tasks than are governmental intelligence organizations.

Particularly in the area of open source (OSINT) collection and processing, the government's best option may be to rely entirely on commercial providers while using dedicated organic resources only for the most difficult or sensitive tasks. One often used statistic is that 80 percent of useful intelligence information comes from "open sources."[74] OSINT advocates have long asserted that private enterprise should play a larger role in collection and analysis of these data. The thrust of their argument is that private enterprise is far better equipped with cutting-edge technology to collect, manage, and interpret large amounts of unformatted data. A recent article on OSINT processing argued that the "Intelligence Community must organize its own technical resources and tap those of the private sector to exploit the latest technology for OSINT collection, analysis, production, and dissemination... [in order to] benefit from smarter search engines, enhanced machine-assisted translation software, and better tools for incorporating audio and video streams into intelligence reports."[75]

Likewise, many privatization advocates claim that the commercial sector is far better equipped to deal with the challenges of the new threat paradigm. Traditional military intelligence methodologies, with their focus on order of battle analysis, indications and warnings, and threat-based technical measures, are unable to gather the information needed to fight trans-national terrorism and other unconventional threats. For counter-terrorism intelligence analysis much of the most useful information is likely to come from collection on financial transactions, web-based communications, and analysis

---

[72] To remedy this situation, the WMD Commission findings recommended that the new DNI play a more active role in identifying and acquiring commercial technologies that could be effectively integrated into collection and analytical processes. Commission on the Intelligence Capabilities of the United States Regarding Weapons of Mass Destruction, Washington DC: GPO (31 March 2005), 326. URL: < http://www.state.gov/t/np/rls/fs/29153.htm>. accessed 15 March 2005.

[73] "Relevant Information: A New Approach to Collection, Sharing and Analysis," 11.

[74] The exact origin of this estimate is uncertain. The figure first appeared in the 1996, "In from the Cold: The Report of the Twentieth Century Fund Task Force on the Future of U.S. Intelligence," but the original source was not cited. The figure is so frequently mentioned in OSINT texts that is has come to be accepted as "fact" but many intelligence experts remain skeptical of this estimate.

[75] Stephen C. Mercado, "Sailing the Sea of OSINT in the Information Age," *Studies in Intelligence: Journal of the American Intelligence Professional* 48, no. 3 (2004): 55.

of large volumes of unformatted and often unclassified text and data. The advanced processing techniques needed for this type of collection and analysis is more highly refined in the day-to-day business of private sector enterprise.

Don Goldstein, a technology researcher at the Institute for Defense Analysis, notes that commercial enterprise is generally far ahead of government in applying the automated, data processing techniques needed for counter-terrorism analysis.[76] The financial community in particular is better equipped to use analytical techniques for parsing large amounts of unformatted data, using automated information extraction methods, and conducting advanced link analysis. Private enterprise also leads in the development of new techniques for computational linguistics and machine automated translation that will be critical for cataloging and analyzing vast amounts of unformatted data from written and digital records. Very few governmental intelligence organizations will be capable of capitalizing on these specialized tools without the significant integration of commercial support. Looking to the future of cutting edge analytical and processing tools, Goldstein notes, "Google is the best thing out there." In order to meet the critical information needs of policymakers and military commanders, the Intelligence Community will increasingly need to exploit the best tools, technology, and services of private providers.

---

[76] Don Goldstein, Institute for Defense Analysis, Science and Technology Division, telephone interview by the author, 5 November 2004.

THE LEGAL AND REGULATORY ENVIRONMENT FOR COMMERCIALIZED INTELLIGENCE AUGMENTATION

Since the Revolutionary War era the U.S. government has made extensive use of private interests for the purpose of gathering and analyzing intelligence data, but governmental transformations of the last decade have brought a significant expansion of the role that private enterprise plays in the collection, analysis, and production of intelligence information. This process has been encouraged by legislative and regulatory changes that have significantly liberalized acquisition and procurement law and facilitated the entry of private enterprise into intelligence fields.

The legal precedents for contracting intelligence support services are clearly outlined in existing statutes and regulations. Executive Order 12333 provides intelligence agencies with broad authority to "enter into contracts or arrangements for the provision of goods or services with private companies or institutions," and to conceal the sponsorship of these contracts for security purposes.[77] These general contracting powers extend to military commanders by Title 10 of the U.S. Code and provide the Secretary of Defense with the authority to engage in commercial activities for support of intelligence-related collection activities abroad.[78]

Despite these clear authorities, acquisition law and regulation remains somewhat vague on how such commercial enterprises should be employed and monitored. With the significant expansion of commercial intelligence augmentation in support of GWOT operations, several key elements of contract law have recently come under increased scrutiny. Legal issues relating to the performance of inherently government functions, the use of personal services contracts, and legal oversight of contract personnel have all come into question as the IC has rapidly expanded private sector augmentation.

INHERENTLY GOVERNMENTAL FUNCTIONS

Although the basic authority for the government to contract for intelligence services is clear, ambiguities in government acquisition policy leave many specifics open to broad interpretation. One of the most debated issues concerning intelligence contracting has been the policy regarding definitions of "inherently governmental functions." For general government contracting, the statutory reference for commercial activities is Office of Management and Budget (OMB) Circular A-76. This document sets forth guidelines for determining "inherently governmental functions" that must be performed only by federal employees. In general, those activities related to "the act of governing"

---

[77] U.S. President, Executive Order 12333, "United States Intelligence Activities," 4 December 1981, 2.7.
[78] 10 U.S.C. § 431. Intelligence Commercial Activities.

and "intimately related to the public interest" are withheld from commercial activity.[79] As described in OMB Circular A-76, these activities include the

> management of Government programs requiring value judgments, as in direction of the national defense; management and direction of the Armed Services; activities performed exclusively by military personnel who are subject to deployment in a combat support or combat service support role...[and the] direction of intelligence and counter-intelligence operations.[80]

Though seemingly clear, the interpretation of this statute has been a matter of some debate within Congress, DoD, and among intelligence professionals.

In August of 2000, the Assistant Secretary of the Army attempted to clarify this restriction. At that time a determination was made to draw legal distinctions for different levels of war, finding that "at the tactical level, the intelligence functions and the operational control of the Army performed by military in the operating forces is an inherently governmental function barred from private sector performance."[81] But the memorandum stipulated that "at the operational and strategic level, the intelligence function performed by military personnel and federal civilian employees is a non-inherently governmental function that should be exempted from private sector performance on the basis of risk to national security from relying on contractors to perform this function."[82]

This decision left open the possibility of the use of contract employees for non-tactical functions but cited legal and security concerns, noting that the

> contract administration oversight exerted over contractors is very different from the command and control exerted over military and civilian employees. Therefore, reliance on private contractors poses risks to maintaining adequate civilian oversight of intelligence operations. Civilian oversight over intelligence operations and technologies is essential to assure intelligence operations are conducted with adequate security safeguards, and within the scope of law and direction of the authorized chain of command and officials.[83]

The equivocal wording of the policy ultimately left open the possibility of private sector providers "to be used to facilitate the gathering or interpretation of intelligence information, in circumstances where contractors are the sole source of a particular capability."[84]

---

[79] Office of Management and Budget, "Federal Acquisition Regulation, Circular No. A-76," 4 August 1983 (revised 1999), URL: <*http://www.whitehouse.gov/omb/circulars/a076/a076.html*>, accessed 25 August 2004.

[80] Circular No., A-76, 3.

[81] Patrick T. Henry, Assistant Secretary of the Army, "Intelligence Exemption Memorandum for the Assistant Deputy Chief of Staff for Intelligence," 26 December 2000, 1

[82] Henry, 2.

[83] Henry, 2.

[84] Henry, 2

With the enormous intelligence demands related to GWOT operations, the policies governing private sector involvement have been broadly interpreted within DoD. Since 9/11, significant shortfalls of intelligence personnel have led to the extensive use of contract employees for intelligence operations in Bosnia, Afghanistan, Iraq, and Guantanamo Bay. Compounding this policy dilemma, many contract employees are operating in environments where the distinctions between levels of war are either vague or entirely irrelevant. A clear example of the blurring of these lines was seen in the much-publicized use of contract interrogators at the Abu Ghraib detention facility in Iraq. In that setting, contract employees were performing similar tactical-level interrogation tasks as their uniformed counterparts. The subsequent Army investigation noted that "the general policy of not contracting for intelligence functions and services was designed in part to avoid many of the problems that eventually developed at Abu Ghraib."[85]

The fallout from the incidents at Abu Ghraib has led to some reconsideration of the definitions of "inherently governmental" operational intelligence functions. A recent memorandum from the Army G-2 (Deputy Chief of Staff for Intelligence) clarified this distinction for the conduct of counter-intelligence operations.[86] The revised policy clearly defines the "direction and control" of CI operations as an inherently governmental function but leaves open several potential activities to commercial providers, including translation/interpretation, analysis, data input, and the production of CI related products.

In the aftermath of the Abu Ghraib revelations, the issue of contractors performing critical security and intelligence functions also gained attention in Congress. In April 2004, Senator Christopher Dodd (D-CT) was joined by several other senate Democrats expressing concern that private military firms were performing "security-related functions" but that "these companies remain largely unregulated."[87] Dodd sent an open letter to the U.S. Comptroller requesting a GAO report on the use, regulation, oversight, and accountability of contract personnel performing operational intelligence and security-related tasks in forward-deployed combat locations.

Later in June Dodd proposed an amendment to bar the use of civilian contractors as military interrogators.[88] The Senate voted against the amendment along party lines (54-43) but even some Republicans voting against the measure expressed their concern over the increasing role of private contractors working in sensitive intelligence related operations. Senator John McCain (R-AZ), stated "ultimately, I believe that interrogations and other functions should be conducted by uniformed personnel,

---

[85] AR 15-6 *Investigation of the Abu Ghraib Detention Facility and 205th Military Intelligence Brigade*, 49.

[86] LTG Keith B. Alexander, Army G-2 (Deputy Chief of Staff for Intelligence), "Memorandum: Contractor Support to Army Counterintelligence," 10 June 2004.

[87] Christopher Dodd, Russell Feingold, Jack Reed, Patrick Leahy, and Jon Corzine, letter to David M. Walker, Comptroller General of the United States, subject: "Dodd Requests GAO Report on Private Military Firms in Iraq, 29 April 2004" URL: <*http://dodd.senate.gov/press/Releases/04/0429.htm*>, accessed 11 March 2005.

[88] "Measure Banning Private Sector Interrogations fails in Senate." *GOVEXEC.com Daily Briefing*, online ed., 16 June 2004, URL: <*http://www.govexec.com/dailyfed/0604/061604cdpm4.htm*>, accessed 22 October 2004.

working directly for the United States government and subject to the web of rules that governs military personnel."[89]

The issue reemerged in the 2005 Defense Authorization Act. The final legislation included language requiring the Secretary of Defense to report on DoD management practices for contractor personnel supporting deployed forces. Among the specific items addressed in the amendment was the establishment of categories of intelligence functions considered inherently governmental and those that "although not inherently governmental functions, should not ordinarily be performed by contractors."[90] A final determination of DoD policy on these activities is forthcoming. One positive aspect of the recent controversy will presumably be some clarification of the operational boundaries for deployed contractors performing these intelligence related activities.

PERSONAL SERVICES CONTRACTING

Another area of concern relating to contract law and intelligence support is the expanding use of personal services contracting.[91] Functions considered "personal services" are those contracts that create an employer-employee type relationship between the contractor personnel and government supervisor. They often include services that are applied directly in support of an organization's integral functions, any services requiring direct supervision to ensure adequate protection of government interest, or the performance of services directly comparable to that of permanent civil service personnel.[92] Under most circumstances there are strict statutory restrictions on the government's use of these contract types.

An analysis of the intelligence support functions currently performed by many commercial providers suggests that most of these contracts are in fact providing "personal services," but various exceptions to acquisition law have permitted their use. The Federal Acquisition Regulation provides for the case-by-case short-term contracting of "individual experts or consultants" in place of civil servants.[93] Furthermore, many of the contracts for intelligence

---

[89] Elaine M. Grossman, "Possible Interrogation Contractor Influence Cited in Senate Vote," *Inside the Pentagon*, online edition, 24 June 2004, URL: *<http://www.d-n-i.net/grossman/contractor_influence_cited. htm>*, accessed 22 October 2004.

[90] U.S. Congress, House, Ronald W. Reagan National Defense Authorization Act for Fiscal Year 2005. 108th Cong., 2nd sess., 20 January 2004, H.R. 4200, URL: *<http://www.wifcon.com/dodauth05.htm>*, accessed 11 November 2004.

[91] Between 1986 and 2001 the percentage of federal procurement funds going toward service contracting rose from 31 to 51 percent. Steven L. Schooner, "Contractor Atrocities at Abu Ghraib: Compromised Accountability in a Streamlined, Outsourced Government" *Stanford Law and Policy Review 16*, no. 2 (2005). Abstract available at URL: *<http://papers.ssrn.com/sol3/papers.cfm?abstract_id=605367>*, accessed 23 November 2004.

[92] For the case of DoD, this refers to civilian personnel governed under U.S. Code Title 10.

[93] FAR, Chapter 37.104 (f) states, that "Personal services contracts for the services of individual experts or consultants are limited by the Classification Act. In addition, the Office of Personnel Management has established requirements which apply in acquiring the personal services of experts or consultants in this manner."

support have been written for services performed outside the United States, which provides other exceptions to domestic acquisition regulation. A recent FAR rule change has granted DoD much greater latitude in using these contract types, now permitting "personal services contracts to be performed outside the United States or that directly support the mission of a DoD intelligence or counter-intelligence organization."[94]

Legislative changes in acquisition law have come about in part to help DoD contend with critical shortages of intelligence personnel. The Senate Intelligence committee report on the 2004 Intelligence Authorization bill specifically cited the need for greater liberalization of contract authority in order for DoD to meet the unanticipated intelligence demands of the Global War on Terror, noting that

> Intelligence Community elements of DoD frequently have a temporary need for additional personnel with specific expertise to meet unanticipated, yet significant, operational requirements that necessitate a bolstering of organizational and personnel efforts created by world events. Current examples include experts on al-Qa'ida, the countries of the Middle East, chemical and biological warfare, and Islamic militant personalities, along with linguists to support interrogation of detainees and review of captured documents. Under current law, U.S. Government agencies generally must choose between hiring additional personnel as government employees or contracting for their services under the restrictive provisions for the temporary or intermittent employment of experts and consultants under section 3109 of title 5, United States Code. The Committee provides relief from these more restrictive authorities by granting authority for Intelligence Community elements of DoD to award personal services contracts notwithstanding any other provision of law....This provision will optimize the capabilities of Intelligence Community elements of DoD in the performance of their roles in the global war on terrorism and in the execution of future national security missions.[95]

While this liberalization of contract authority certainly helps to bolster short-term capabilities beyond resources available within the permanent civil service, this type of contracting vehicle does present added challenges for contract management. As commercial providers increasingly fulfill an employee-like relationship to the government there is a much greater burden for close contract management by the operational chain of command. Even with personal services contracts there are significant limitations governing the manner in which contract personnel are managed and supervised. Intelligence leaders are increasingly challenged by operational environments in which employees are subject to varying standards of conduct, accountability, and legal responsibility. This is particularly true since military commanders may possess far different legal authority in dealing with contract

---

[94] "Interim Rule to the Defense Federal Acquisition Regulation Supplement (DFARS): Personal Services Contracts," *Federal Register 69*, no. 180 (17 September 2004): 55991. URL: <*http://www.acq.osd.mil/ dpap/dars/dfars/changenotice/*>, accessed 3 November 2004.

[95] U.S. Congress, Senate, *Conference Committee Comments on Fiscal Year 2004 Intelligence Authorization Bill and Other Matters*, S. 108-044, 108th Cong., 2nd sess., 8 May 2003, URL: <*http://www. fas.org/irp/congress/2003_rpt/srpt108-44.html*>, accessed 17 March 2005.

employees than government intelligence personnel. These supervisory challenges are important considerations as leaders consider the extent to which private sector services will be integrated into forward-deployed operational capabilities.

LEGAL OVERSIGHT

In addition to questions over inherently governmental functions and the use of personnel services contracts, there are important considerations regarding the legal oversight and jurisdiction over contract intelligence support. Previous legal decisions have challenged UCMJ jurisdiction over civilians in peacetime overseas environments. Generally these exceptions have been extended to government contractors thereby restricting the use of disciplinary trials by courts-martial and use of other non-judicial punishment.[96]

Theoretically, the Military Extraterritorial Jurisdiction Act (MEJA) places military contractors operating overseas under clear U.S. legal jurisdiction, but the incidents at Abu Ghraib have highlighted some important limitations of this law. Several of the contracts for intelligence support in Iraq were not awarded under DoD contracting authority and therefore not be subject to the MEJA.[97] Furthermore, the MEJA only applies to U.S. citizens and at least two of the linguist contractors implicated in the abuse incidents at Abu Ghraib were non-U.S. citizens and therefore exempt from prosecution under the law. In the case of Iraq, the Coalition Provisional Authority also has an agreement with the interim Iraq government granting immunity to private contractors from prosecution under local law.

The combination of overlapping authorities has highlighted several deficiencies in the MEJA recently raised in congressional debate over private contract support for coalition forces in Iraq. Responding to these concerns in May of 2004, Congressman Marty Meehan (D-MA) introduced the Contractor Accountability Act intended to tighten the government's jurisdiction over contractors working for the U.S. government overseas.[98] Meehan, a member of both the House Armed Services and the Judiciary Committees, has been a vocal critic of the Iraq war and repeatedly called for strengthening accountability of DoD contractors and improving interrogation policies in light of the Abu Ghraib incidents. Although the exact language of Meehan's amendment was not included as part of the 2005 Defense Authorization Act, several additional provisions on contractor oversight were included in the final legislation. The revised bill appears to have corrected the previous deficiencies and now extends

---

[96] For a discussion of case law establishing this precedent, see MAJ Joseph R. Perlak, USA, "The Military Extraterritorial Jurisdiction Act of 2000: Implications for Contractor Personnel," *Military Law Review* 169 (September 2001), 92-140.

[97] AR 15-6 *Investigation of the Abu Ghraib Detention Facility*, 50.

[98] Marty Meehan, "Meehan Introduces Legislation to Increase Private Contractor Accountability," *U.S. House of Representatives Press Release*, 18 May 2004. URL: <*http://www.house.gov/apps/list/press/ma05_ meehan/NR040518IraqContractors.html*>, accessed 11 March 2005.

the MEJA to contractor employees working for all federal agencies supporting DoD missions overseas.[99]

Although a strengthened MEJA should resolve clear-cut cases of criminal conduct with contract employees, there still is some concern over what powers a commander may utilize for corrective punishment and matters of non-criminal order and discipline. Contract employees are generally subject only to the terms and conditions of the contract language. In most cases this excludes contractors from UCMJ and non-judicial punishments that military commanders regularly apply to active duty soldiers and some deployed civil service employees. This exercise of command prerogative is even more critical for leaders directing combat operations or dealing with the performance of sensitive intelligence functions. The Army investigation of Abu Ghraib specifically cited the liability associated with limitations of such traditional command powers:

> Performing the interrogation function in-house with government employees has several tangible benefits. It enables the Army more readily to manage the function if all personnel are directly and clearly subject to the chain of command, and other administrative and/or criminal sanctions, and it allows the function to be directly accessible by the commander/supervisor without going through a Contracting Officer Representative.[100]

The circumstances at Abu Ghraib are not unique. Several individuals interviewed for this study noted similar examples of ambiguities in legal status for deployed non-governmental employees and frequent uncertainty as to the authority of the chain of command over contractors. A 2003 GAO report on DoD contract management procedures reinforced this finding. This review of overseas support contracts found significant inconsistencies in contract language pertaining to the general discipline of contractor personnel, adherence to force protection requirements, and enforcement of published General Orders.[101] These findings highlight the pressing need for clear legal authority over contractors serving intelligence support missions. Ambiguous legal guidelines in contract language could be a particular liability for intelligence support personnel who may be subject to unique security, counter-intelligence, and force protection requirements.

Recent rules changes in the applicable Defense Federal Acquisition Regulation (DFAR) have attempted to clarify some of these authorities, stipulating that contract employees are required to comply with U.S. and host-country law, as well as applicable treaties and international agreements. Likewise, a DFAR revision explicitly states that contractors must comply with all "orders, directives, and instructions issued by the Combatant Commander relating to force protection, security, health, safety or

---

[99] U.S. Congress, House. *Ronald W. Reagan National Defense Authorization Act for Fiscal Year 2005.* 108th Cong., 2nd sess., 20 January 2004. H.R. 4200, SEC. 1088. URL: < *http://www.wifcon.com/dodauth05. htm* >, accessed 11 November 2004.

[100] AR 15-6 *Investigation of the Abu Ghraib Detention Facility*, 49.

[101] Government Accountability Office, *Military Operations: Contractors Provide Vital Services to Deployed Forces but are Not Adequately Addressed in DOD Plans,* GAO-03-695 (June 2003), URL: <*http://www.gao.gov/highlights/d03695high.pdf*>, accessed 13 October 2004, 28.

relations and interactions with local nationals."[102] The new rules also reinforce the existing authority of Contracting Officers to direct vendors to remove any personnel "who jeopardize or interfere with mission accomplishment."[103] Although this authority was established by previous regulation, several commanders involved with incidents of contractor misconduct at Abu Ghraib were apparently unaware of such authorities for dealing with violations by contract employees.

OTHER LEGAL CONSIDERATIONS

The previous discussion described just a few of the important legal issues relating to the management of commercial intelligence augmentation but several other potential concerns have not yet been sufficiently addressed. As private corporations rush to provide support to intelligence and security operations there remain significant questions concerning the control, retention, use, and proliferation of proprietary intelligence information that contractors may acquire while working for government organizations.

The Law of Armed Conflict clearly establishes the concept of state monopoly on the application of deadly force but is less clear on how the government can extend such authority over the control of sensitive intelligence information. Of particular concern is how unmonitored subcontractors might potentially take their acquired knowledge to other commercial ventures or even to foreign employment. For many intelligence support contracts there appear to be few mechanisms for monitoring the use of proprietary data and knowledge after contract termination. These concerns also extend to the potential collection and retention of sensitive data on U.S. persons and foreign citizens by private firms. As Sen. Patrick Leahy (D-VT) observed in a recent public statement on the need for improved regulation of intelligence service providers, "new technologies, new private-pubic domestic security partnerships, and the rapid rise of giant information brokers...have all combined to produce powerful new threats to privacy."[104] Leahy noted that under current contract law and regulation "very little is known about the integrity and handling of this information, and there are insufficient rules and oversight to protect public privacy."[105]

Another issue of potential legal concern is the status of intelligence contractors under international law. Commercial contractors are now involved in nearly every stage of the intelligence cycle, including critical collection management and technical analysis functions, yet the status of non-uniformed contract personnel remains somewhat unclear under international law.

---

[102] "Defense Federal Acquisition Regulation Supplement; Contractor Personnel Supporting a Force Deployed Outside the United States," 48 CFR Part 252.225-7040 (d), *Federal Register 70*, no. 86 (5 May 2005). URL: *<http://frwebgate1.access.gpo.gov/cgibin/waisgate.cgi?WAISdocID=00205819834+0+0+0 &WAISaction=retrieve>*, accessed 11 May 2005.

[103] "Defense Federal Acquisition Regulation Supplement; Contractor Personnel Supporting a Force Deployed Outside the United States," 48 CFR Part 252.225-7040 (h).

[104] Roman Kupchinsky, "*Information Revolution Feeds Alternative Intelligence Market,*" Radio Free Europe/Radio Liberty, 23 May 2005, URL: *<http://www.rferl.org/featuresarticle/2005/05/e1dc62e7-504a-4abb-a61f-008f7167bfab.html>*, accessed 3 June 2005.

[105] Kupchinsky.

Generally speaking, civilians accompanying armed forces in declared wars are considered non-combatants but entitled to protected status as prisoners of war in case of capture. Contract employees are not entitled to take part in "hostilities" but may still be held liable under international law for participation in acts later determined to be war crimes. The DFAR stipulates that contract personnel "shall not undertake any role that would jeopardize their status [as a non-combatant]" and "shall not use force or otherwise directly participate in acts likely to cause actual harm to enemy armed forces."[106] This restriction may be clear enough for functions such as logistics but is somewhat more ambiguous for private contractors supporting operational intelligence functions. This ambiguity leaves open significant questions regarding the personal liability of contractors performing intelligence functions that directly support interrogations, security operations, or offensive targeting decisions.[107]

There also remains some question as to the potential liability of the firms employing contract workers accused of criminal misconduct. There are currently two civil suits filed on behalf of several Iraqi detainees against Titan Corporation and CACI, firms supplying contract interrogators at Abu Ghraib.[108] One of the cases was filed by the widow of a detainee who died in custody following an interrogation by a contract employee at the detention facility. The outcome of these cases may have significant impact on the manner in which civilian contractors may be employed for future intelligence support missions.

A final concern is the matter of values. Certainly, great public trust and expectation are granted to intelligence professionals serving the public interest and protecting the nation's critical security operations. It is reasonable to consider whether private entrepreneurs may be expected to adhere to similar systems of values and conduct. A "duty concept" cannot easily be codified into contract language, nor can an implicit ethical system be easily enforced through acquisition law. A basic question that must be considered by policymakers is whether the institutional values guiding the intelligence profession are consistent with the profit motives of private corporations whose interests necessarily reflect those of private shareholders. This inquiry does not presuppose a lack of dedication or values on the part of individual contractors but it does suggest some inherent risks associated with relying upon private corporations for critical intelligence functions.

These issues suggest that many critical questions regarding the use of contract intelligence support remain unanswered. Complex legal, regulatory, and ethical issues have yet to be sufficiently addressed by policymakers, particularly as commercial activities become even more integrated into all aspects of intelligence operations.

---

[106] "Defense Federal Acquisition Regulation Supplement; Contractor Personnel Supporting a Force Deployed Outside the United States," 48 CFR Part 252.225-7040(b).

[107] For a brief discussion of contractor status under international law, see Jennifer Elsea, *U.S. Treatment of Prisoners in Iraq: Selected Legal Issues,* CRS Report for Congress, 24 May 2004.

[108] *Al Rawi v. Titan Corp.,* No. 04 CV 1143 (S.D. Cal. June 9, 2004) and *Ibrahim v Titan Corp.,* No 1:04 CV 01248 (D.C.D July 27, 2004). Michael J. Grinfeld, "War Incorporated," *California Lawyer* (May 2005), 25.

EVALUATIVE FRAMEWORK FOR COMMERCIALIZED
INTELLIGENCE AUGMENTATION

In order for Community leaders to make appropriate determinations concerning the use of commercial augmentation for intelligence support functions, careful consideration must be given to the suitability of private sector involvement. For operational needs to be satisfied and public interest adequately protected there must be assurance that certain baseline performance criteria can be met within the terms of the contract partnership. The following framework is offered to assist Intelligence Community leaders in decisions regarding the applicability of integrating commercial services into an organization's operational functions. These evaluative criteria are not intended to be a definitive guideline for determining the suitability of commercial integration but serve to highlight some fundamental elements that are necessary for the effective integration and management of commercial augmentation programs.

This framework offers some baseline evaluative criteria in three general areas: the acceptability of private sector involvement, the suitability of vendor services, and accountability of contract management procedures. Each of these criteria must be satisfied to ensure the effective use of commercial augmentation. As demonstrated in the following case studies, shortfalls in any aspect of this framework can lead to ineffective integration of commercial services, poor contract administration, and compromise of government interest. Careful consideration of these criteria is necessary to establish an effective partnership between government and private sector providers.

Proposed Evaluative Criteria for Determining
the Applicability of Commercialized
Intelligence Augmentation

Acceptability of Private Sector Involvement

- Contract service does not perform inherently governmental functions.
- Contract administration adheres to proper solicitation and award procedures.
- Contract service does not undermine operational security.
- Vendor offers a best value alternative (including price and performance standards).

Suitability of Vendor Services

- Vendor offers unique services or products unavailable in the public sector.
- Vendor offers scalability of service and flexible output to meet mission requirements.
- Contract is negotiated in a mature market environment with in-sector competition.
- Bidder offers past performance record and known reliability.

Accountability of Contract Management Procedures

- Contract language offers clear legal oversight and accountability measures.
- Contract offers clear Statement of Work (SOW) and evaluation procedures.
- Contract provides effective integration plan and clear performance measures.
- Government possesses sufficiently trained, on-site contract management personnel.

EVALUATING PUBLIC-PRIVATE INTELLIGENCE PARTNERSHIPS: SELECTED CASE STUDIES

The following case studies reflect recent experiments with public-private intelligence support partnerships. These examples demonstrate a broad range of commercialization initiatives currently used within the Intelligence Community. These examples are by no means an exhaustive list of intelligence privatization programs. They offer a broad overview of various commercialization efforts and test the utility of the evaluative framework by demonstrating the challenges associated with developing and administering effective contractual relationships with private sector providers.[109]

PRIVATIZED PERSONNEL SECURITY INVESTIGATIONS

One of the most important elements of the nation's counterintelligence effort is the investigation and screening of government employees and contractors. Traditionally, these investigative services have been performed by trained government agents employed by the Office of Personnel Management (OPM) and the Defense Security Service (DSS). The DSS conducts the majority of the clearance investigations for Department of Defense civilian employees, military service members, and Pentagon contractors.

Like other DoD organizations during the 1990s, the DSS experienced significant staffing reductions amounting to a 40 percent overall cut in personnel levels in the decade after 1989.[110] This personnel drawdown led to increasing backlogs of security investigations and growing concerns over the effectiveness of the nation's counterintelligence program in the wake of several high-profile espionage cases during the 1990s. Responding to this crisis in 1996, the Deputy Secretary of Defense directed the use of commercial augmentation to improve efficiency and quality of investigations and reduce backlogged caseload. As part of this program, OPM initiated a privatization initiative through the establishment of the U.S. Investigation Services (USIS), an Employee Stock Ownership Corporation chartered to conduct personnel security investigations on behalf of the government.

This privatization effort was intended to infuse greater flexibility into the investigative labor pool, achieve savings through reductions in civil service benefits, and bring greater efficiency through commercial automation.[111] The final clearance adjudication process was retained as a strictly governmental function within DSS and

---

[109] See Appendix for a consolidated overview of the case study evaluations based upon selected criteria.

[110] U.S. Department of Defense, Office of the Inspector General, *Statement of Donald Mancuso, Deputy Inspector General Department of Defense before the Senate Armed Services Committee, Hearing to review procedures and standards for the granting of security clearances at the Department of Defense* (6 April 2000). URL: <*http://www.fas.org/sgp/congress/2000/mancuso.html.*>, accessed 2 May 2005.

[111] For a brief review of the initial cost analysis of OPM privatization, see Government Accountability Office, *Cost Analysis: Privatizing OPM Investigations*, (5 July 1996) GAO/66D-96-121R.

OPM but much of the investigative work was outsourced to private sector providers. The policy of contracting out for these investigations was intended to permit organizations like DSS and OPM to more easily "right-size" their personnel levels based upon variable demand for service, a task difficult to achieve under restrictive civil service employment regulations.

Thus far this transition to partial privatization has not produced all of the intended results. Several years into the privatization effort a 1999 GAO report found that significant numbers of personnel security investigations remained incomplete or were not adjudicated in a timely manner.[112] A subsequent Joint Military Intelligence College study on the privatization program cited security concerns with contract investigative support, suggesting that the system of commercial augmentation lacked sufficient measures to ensure "accountability, integrity and confidentiality" of critical counterintelligence functions.[113] A concurrent GAO study of DSS investigations revealed repeated lapses in the thoroughness of background screenings, noting that the "vast majority" of examined investigations failed to comply with federal quality control standards. The GAO report concluded that "in an effort to streamline operations and improve efficiency [DSS] relaxed its investigative guidance, eliminated key quality control mechanisms, [and] inadequately trained its investigators."[114] The study determined that these deficiencies resulted from "ineffective management reforms... undertaken as reinvention efforts ostensibly based on the National Performance Review, which called for improving government at less cost. However, DSS's actions did not achieve this result."[115]

---

[112] Government Accountability Office. DOD Personnel: *Inadequate Personnel Security Investigations Pose National Security Risks,* GAO/NSIAD-00-12 (October 1999). URL: <*http://www.gao.gov/ archive/2000/ns00065t.pdf*>, accessed 13 November 2004.

[113] CPT William Colligan, USA, *The Privatization of Personnel Security: The Effects of the National Performance Review on the Intelligence Community,* MSSI Thesis, Washington, DC: Joint Military Intelligence College, 2000.

[114] Government Accountability Office, *Inadequate Personnel Security Investigations Pose National Security Risks,* Statement of Carol R. Schuster, Associate Director, National Security Preparedness Issues, National Security and International Affairs Division, Testimony before the Subcommittee on National Security, Veterans Affairs, and International Relations, GAO/T-NSIAD-00-65, 16 February 2000. URL: <*http://www.gao.gov/archive/2000/ns00065t.pdf*>, accessed 9 March 2005.

[115] Schuster statement.

Is Implementation of the NPR Always Feasible?[116]

In a case study about the NPR, *The Privatization of Personnel Security: The Effects of the National Performance Review on the Intelligence Community,* William E. Colligan identifies the arguments for and against the privatization of personnel security functions through the eyes of both the entrepreneurs and the public administrators. He analyzes action by the Clinton administration to privatize the Office of Federal Investigations, an arm of the Office of Personnel Management (OPM), which handled about 30 percent of all background investigations for the U.S. Government. The key point addressed: Should the government continue to privatize its personnel security functions and responsibilities?

Colligan established a formula to consider a personnel security system, evaluating **accountability, integrity,** and **confidentiality**. The specific example used is a case study of the operation of the newly created U.S. Investigative Services (USIS) to assess the feasibility and desirability of the government's efforts at personnel security privatization. Colligan found USIS weak in all these elements, and recommended against using private enterprise to conduct background investigations.

Since that time, the outsourcing of investigations has significantly increased. In July 2004 OPM awarded a multi-million dollar blanket purchase agreement to five separate private companies for investigative services.[117] DSS also significantly expanded its commercial augmentation program by shifting much of its excess caseload to several private sector providers.[118] Yet this transition to privatized investigations has not resolved the persistent problem of caseload backlog. A recent 2004 GAO report on DSS operations estimated the current backlog of clearance applications to be approximately 188,000.[119] Additionally, OPM and DSS earned repeated criticism for questionable investigative standards, processing inefficiency, and poor management oversight.[120]

Ironically, the GAO determined that the federal and private sector workforce itself was a primary factor causing investigative backlogs - precisely the problem the

---

[116] Colligan, *Privatization of Personnel Security.*

[117] Calvin Biesecker, "OMP Selects Five Contractors to Expand Capacity for Background Checks," *Defense Daily,* online ed., 28 July 2004, URL: <*http://web.lexis-nexis.com/universe/document*>, accessed 21 September 2004. The BPA contract was awarded to CACI International, Marsh and McLennan's Kroll Government Services, ManTech-MSM, Omniplex World Services Corp., and Systems Application and Technology.

[118] Defense Security Service (DSS) Augmentation Programs, Web-only document, URL: <www.dss.mil/aboutdss/augmentation>, accessed 17 September 2004. In January 2003 DSS awarded three personnel investigation contracts to Dyncorp-CSC, ManTech-ISJV, and Omniplex World Services.

[119] Shane Harris, "Defense Department Lacks Staff to Tackle Security Clearance Backlog," GOVEXEC.com, online ed., 27 May 2004, URL: <*http://www.govexec.com/dailyfed/0504/052704h1.htm*>, accessed 21 September 2004.

[120] A sampling of recent GAO reports provides some idea of the ongoing issues. "DOD Needs to Overcome Impediments to Eliminating Backlog and Determining Its Size," February 2004; "More Consistency Needed in Determining Eligibility for Top Secret Security Clearances," April 2001; "More Accurate Estimate of Overdue Security Clearance Reinvestigations Is Needed," September 2000; "More Actions Needed to Address Backlog of Security Clearance Reinvestigations," August 2000; "Inadequate Personnel Security Investigations Pose National Security Risks," February 2000.

privatization program was intended to resolve. Currently, most contracted investigators are employed on a part-time basis and are therefore not always available to satisfy surged caseload requirements. OPM's primary contractor recently reported the addition of nearly 100 investigators per month to address increased caseload demand but admitted a turnover in personnel amounting to 70 employees per month.[121] Likewise, DSS's contract partners recently expressed reluctance to hire more permanent staff, stating "that they would incur additional financial risk if they were to use full-time investigators,"[122] in place of part-time labor.

Although privatization was intended to infuse greater flexibility into the labor force, the government is now facing the unintended consequence of not having an assured resource base of trained investigators to meet unanticipated increases in demand. A recent report noted that "DSS has fallen so far behind because its investigators cannot accurately project the size of future workload, making it almost impossible to plan accurately for future budget and workforce size requirements."[123]

These persistent investigative delays and quality control issues were addressed in the 2004 Intelligence Reform Act, which requires the selection of a single executive agency to direct the "day to day oversight of investigations and adjudication for personnel security clearances."[124] The new legislation stipulated a goal of 120 days for final determination of 80 percent of all clearance applications, as well as the establishment of uniform investigative standards and requirements for all government background investigations. The effectiveness of these measures remains to be seen. Despite several years of experimentation with various privatization programs there remains a significant backlog of investigations and a persistent shortage of investigators.[125] There also remain questions about the accountability, training, management, and oversight of contract personnel conducting background investigations.

APPLYING THE EVALUATIVE CRITERIA

This mixed record of commercial outsourcing for personnel security investigations indicates that privatization is not always a panacea for government inefficiency. Thus far private vendors have fallen short in providing sufficient scalability of service and

---

[121] Government Accountability Office. *DoD Needs to Overcome Impediments to Eliminating Backlog and Determining Its Size*, GAO-04-344 (February 2004). URL: < *http://www.gao.gov/highlights/d04344high. pdf* >, accessed 10 November 2004.

[122] *DoD Needs to Overcome Impediments to Eliminating Backlog and Determining Its Size.*

[123] Caitlin Harrington, "Backlog of Pentagon Security Clearances Nearing 200,000," CQ.com Homeland Security, 26 May 2004, URL: <*http://www.cqhls.com/hs/dislay.do?dockey/cqonline/prod/data/docs/html/ hsnews/108>*, accessed 17 March 2005.

[124] U.S. Congress, House, *Intelligence Reform and Terrorism Prevention Act of 2004*. 108th Cong., 2d sess., 7 December 2004, section 3001, URL <*http://www.c-span.org/pdf/2004IntelAct.pdf>*, accessed 7 March 2005.

[125] *DoD Needs to Overcome Impediments to Eliminating Backlog and Determining Its Size.* Another recent report noted that adjudication time of DSS investigation for Pentagon contract employees has actually increased from 319 days in 2001 to 375 days in 2004. Caitlin Harrington, "Backlog of Pentagon Security Clearances Nearing 200,000."

assured output to meet the government's needs. These shortfalls have occurred in part because vendors have not yet demonstrated a long-term record of performance and reliability. Furthermore, there remains some question as to whether contract employees have received adequate training to satisfy government standards for quality control and operational security.

The government bears responsibility for generally poor integration of commercial services by not providing adequate oversight and contract management procedures. As this case suggests, effective commercial augmentation programs require clear plans for contract surveillance, defined standards for performance and delivery, and carefully considered evaluation metrics to protect government interests and adequately satisfy all operational needs.

COMMERCIAL REMOTE SENSING

Privatization of personnel security investigations evolved as a means for infusing greater flexibility into the government's labor pool. Conversely, a privatization initiative for remote sensing came about primarily from rapid technological advancements in private sector imaging technology.[126] For most of the Cold War the government held a tight monopoly on viable technology for operational-quality remote sensing platforms, but in recent years there has been a significant erosion of this qualitative advantage. As private technology reached near-parity capability with some national collection platforms, there was much greater incentive for government exploitation of commercial products. The operational utility of private sector collectors became clear when commercial satellites recently achieved half-meter resolution for electro-optical imaging.[127] This technical achievement opened the door for experimentation with various outsourcing initiatives to satisfy many intelligence-related requirements.

As a result of these technical advancements, in 2000 an independent commission for the National Imagery and Mapping Agency (now the National Geospatial-Intelligence Agency or NGA) called for greater governmental exploitation of commercial imaging technology. Citing NIMA's laggardly movement on commercial integration, the commission called for "a policy review and coherent strategic direction for the use of (and reliance upon) commercial products."[128] The commission challenged the traditional notion that the production of visual overhead collection and analysis

---

[126] "Remote sensing" is a generic term used to describe a wide range of technical disciplines for observing and measuring terrestrial objects. This term encompasses diverse functions such as electro-optical imaging, Global Positioning System navigation, terrestrial mapping, RADAR, aerial photography, and Landsat multi-spectral imaging.

[127] Among others, the Space Imaging Ikonos 2 satellite has produced 1-meter resolution, while the DigitalGlobe owned QuickBird has 0.6-meter resolution. Marcia S. Smith, *U.S. Space Programs: Civilian, Military, and Commercial,* CRS Report IB92011 (Washington, DC: Library of Congress, Congressional Research Service, 2003), 5.

[128] *The Information Edge: Imagery Intelligence and Geospatial Information in an Evolving National Security Environment,* Report of the Independent Commission on the National Imagery and Mapping Agency (December 2000), URL: *<http://www.fas.org/irp/agency/nima/commission/article02.htm>*, accessed 16 September 2004.

should be a purely governmental function. The final report encouraged NIMA to "commercialize itself" and adopt new business practices to integrate a wider range of private sector tools.[129]

Responding to these recommendations, in 2003 the President's Executive Office of Science and Technology Policy established a directive for the use of commercial remote sensing products. The directive committed the government to "rely to the maximum practical extent on U.S. commercial remote sensing space capabilities for filling imagery and geospatial needs for military, intelligence, foreign policy, homeland security, and civil users."[130] Reflecting this new approach, the most recent Quadrennial Defense Review cited the use of commercial imagery as one of five key emerging technologies that the DoD would exploit "to significantly increase U.S. advantage in intelligence collection, analysis, and security."[131]

This presidential policy initiative directed the development of an explicit strategy for integrating commercial products into military and intelligence applications. The strategy directed that the government determine what operational needs could be reliably met through commercial resources and then communicate these current and projected requirements to industry providers. The directive centralized the acquisition and dissemination process to make NGA the primary agency responsible for managing commercial support. Finally, the initiative encouraged the habitual use of commercial products in order to create "a long-term, sustainable relationship" between the government and private sector providers.[132] Thus, rather than trying to restrict or limit the proliferation of advanced commercial remote sensing, the government became its primary consumer.

With this mandate, the NGA went from being an ad hoc user of commercial resources to a primary consumer. In 2003 the NGA awarded a $500 million contract under its NextView program to Digital Globe for their next generation, .5-meter resolution imaging system.[133] Another NGA contract program, Project Clearview, recently awarded a 5-year agreement with several commercial providers for up to $500 million of imagery purchases.[134]

The value of this commercial integration was clearly demonstrated during the major combat operation phase of OIF. A Joint Lessons Learned study found that the "synergy gained by skillfully combining intelligence from US with commercial space

---

[129] *The Information Edge*, 52.

[130] "U.S. Commercial Remote Sensing Policy Fact Sheet," Office of Science and Technology Policy, Executive Office of the President, 25 April 2003. URL: <*http://www.whitehouse.gov/news/releases/2003/05/20030513-8.html*>, accessed 2 May 2005.

[131] U.S. Department of Defense, *Quadrennial Defense Review: America's Security in the 21st Century* (Washington, DC: Government Printing Office, 2001), 38.

[132] "Remote Sensing Policy Fact Sheet," 2.

[133] "NGA Taps ORBIMAGE for Clearview," *GEO World, Government Connection*, May 2004, URL: <*http://www.geoplace.com/uploads/georeport/040407.htm*>, accessed 16 November 2004.

[134] Frank Sietzen, "A Clearview of NIMA's Commercial Imagery Use," *Geospatial Solutions*, online ed., 1 March 2003, URL: <*http://www.geospatial-online.com/geospatialsolutions/content/jps?id=4*>, accessed 16 September 2004.

assets provided forces, especially CFSOCC (Combined Forces Special Operations Component Commander), with excellent intelligence."[135] The report recommended that NGA continue development programs to acquire commercial products as part of the military's collection management process. The report concluded that "commercial high-resolution, multi-spectral and radar satellite imagery proved to be a valuable, but still under-exploited, resource."[136]

From the government's perspective there several distinct advantages of integrating commercial products into the intelligence planning cycle. The director of NGA, Lt Gen James Clapper (USAF, Ret.), noted that commercial resources are particularly useful as a "gap mitigator" when national technical measures are over-taxed or lack sufficient coverage of a particular area of interest.[137] Clapper explained that commercial augmentation can be used to shift many "routine" requirements away from national technical platforms and permit a focus on high-priority missions and the most technically challenging targets. Additionally, Clapper suggested that the unclassified nature of commercial remote sensing products meant that the government has much greater flexibility to share data with foreign national partners and third-party government entities for use in non-intelligence related applications.[138]

Certainly the noteworthy success of integrating commercial remote sensing products for intelligence use provides optimism for the future of such public-private partnerships. Commercial augmentation holds a major advantage for the government as it may now opt to purchase products for some collection requirements rather than building costly systems for every need. This also has the benefit of reducing capital expenditures from limited acquisition budgets and permitting organizations to utilize Operations and Maintenance funding to satisfy certain collection requirements, in effect "changing the color of money" that may be applied for short-term, high priority missions.

Despite these clear advantages, the use of commercial remote sensing for intelligence operations raises several important questions. Firstly, high-quality commercial imagery products are also potentially available to non-U.S. governmental organizations and other private entities with sufficient monetary resources. This issue of "shutter control" has already become a matter of some concern within the Intelligence Community and was addressed in the President's 2003 remote sensing directive. The policy determined that in some cases "the United States government may restrict operations of the commercial systems in order to limit collection and/or dissemination of certain data and products."[139] As part of its "assured access" agreement with commercial imagery

---

[135] Joint Forces Command, "Joint Lessons Learned: Operation IRAQI FREEDOM Major Combat Operations," unpublished coordinating draft report, 1 March 2004, 67

[136] "Joint Lessons Learned: OIF Major Combat Operations," 67.

[137] Lieutenant General James R. Clapper, (USAF, Ret.), Director, National Geospatial-Intelligence Agency, untitled lecture given at the Joint Military Intelligence College, Distinguished Speaker Program, Washington, DC, 5 December 2004. Comments used with the permission of speaker.

[138] Clapper lecture, 5 December 2004.

[139] "Commercial Remote Sensing Policy Fact Sheet," 3.

providers,[140] NIMA (NGA) paid $1.9 million over 2 months, plus an additional $5 million for other related products during early OEF operations. At the time some press reports accused the agency of using this method to restrict commercial products from public dissemination.[141]

The government has not repeated use of "checkbook shutter control" during OIF but the OEF experience raises interesting questions regarding proprietary control of dual-use commercial technology. When commercial providers have access to sensitive intelligence information or unique technical capabilities there is a compelling government interest in maintaining security and control of that data. This case clearly illustrates the complex challenges for effective contract management as private sector enterprise becomes more and more integrated into U.S. intelligence operations. Clapper noted that as such public-private intelligence partnerships expand, "we must retain a sufficient workforce in the government to oversee what the contract providers do."[142]

Another issue of concern is the viability of commercial providers during periods of reduced government demand. The GWOT has been a boon for commercial remote sensing providers, as well as numerous other intelligence and security related firms. But most Intelligence Community observers suggest that current levels of operational spending will be unsustainable in the long term. As the security situation in Iraq and Afghanistan stabilize, there will be reduced demand for such commercial services and products. This inevitable reduction in demand will be less of a dilemma for service-based providers who can quickly downsize their personnel levels. But for technically oriented, highly capitalized industries such as remote sensing providers, a significant downturn in acquisition by the government may seriously jeopardize their commercial viability. As the government increasingly relies on private sector providers to fulfill critical operational requirements, careful consideration of market maturity and the long-term viability of providers will be appropriate.

APPLYING THE EVALUATIVE CRITERIA

The government's exploitation of cutting-edge private sector remote sensing technology is a prime example of the enormous potential benefits of public-private partnerships for commercialized intelligence augmentation. Through NGA's commercial acquisition program the government has used its contracting powers to acquire needed intelligence products that may be effectively supplied by private

---

[140] Numerous press reports used the term "checkbook shutter control" to describe NGA's purchase agreement with several commercial providers during the initial stages of Operation ENDURING FREEDOM. It should be noted that during a 5 December 2004, JMIC Distinguished Lecture Program, Lt Gen Clapper strongly denied the accusation that NGA's intent was to "control" access by purchasing all available commercial collection capability. Clapper indicated that the NGA purchases were made simply to meet operational requirements — not to corner the market. Clapper suggested that the media had misunderstood the intent of NGA actions. Comments used with the permission of speaker.

[141] Antonio Regalado, "U.S. Allows Dissemination of Satellite Photos of Iraq," *The Wall Street Journal*, 21 March 2003, URL: <*http://www.globalsecurity.org/org/news/2003/030321-iraq-imagery01.htm*>, accessed 16 November 2004.

[142] Clapper lecture, 5 December 2004. Comments used with the permission of speaker.

sector providers. NGA's centralized management process has produced an efficient and rationalized approach to commercial acquisition through established relationships with known and reliable private sector partners. This approach has enabled operational commanders to seamlessly integrate commercial products and technology into their intelligence mission cycle and permitted government resources to be applied elsewhere for mission requirements where commercial services are either unavailable or not suited to operational needs.

Based upon the evaluative criteria there are two main areas of concern with the government's commercial remote sensing program. The first issue is how the government will maintain sufficient operational security over privately produced data in cases where unlimited public distribution may jeopardize U.S. military operations or national security. This issue will only become more problematic as high-resolution commercial imagery becomes widely available to non-governmental entities. The second issue is the viability of the commercial marketplace during periods of reduced government demand and whether the private sector will be able to provide flexible levels of service to meet the variable requirements of the Intelligence Community. Much of the value of commercial augmentation will be lost if private sector providers do establish business models that can accommodate unpredictable government requirements only by maintaining a wider viability in the open marketplace.

COMMERCIALIZED INTELLIGENCE
SUPPORT TO THE GWOT

These two cases of commercial augmentation demonstrate several potential benefits and liabilities. The following analysis offers a somewhat different approach, examining the overall methodology of contract management across the broad range of commercial intelligence support services currently provided to deployed forces in the Global War on Terror. This structured analysis provides an opportunity to examine several key aspects of the acquisition process including contract development and award, management procedures, and quality control measures. This approach is intended to examine several specifically identified shortfalls in current contract management procedures and shows how the evaluative framework may be applied for improved policy decisions on commercial augmentation.

Recent government investigations and information gathered for this study have revealed numerous shortfalls in contract management procedures within the Intelligence Community, particularly the weak oversight of intelligence support contracts for GWOT operations. Some issues cited in recent reports are repeated violations of Federal Acquisition Regulation, misuse of the Federal Supply Schedule, significant performance of out-of-scope activity by contractors, improper use of personal services contracts, and inadequate attention to contract delivery and performance.

A 2004 DoD Inspector General report reviewed a sampling of contract awards for the Iraq Coalition Provisional Authority, including several vendors providing intelligence related support services in Iraq, and found "significant weaknesses" in management procedures for 22 of the 24 contracts reviewed.[143] Another recent review of Department of Interior contracts for intelligence support services in Iraq revealed "a lack of effective management controls" in 10 of 11 task orders worth a total of $66 million.[144] A previous 2003 GAO report on DoD contracting practices, including intelligence operations in the Balkans, Afghanistan, and Iraq, determined that contract oversight was "lacking in key areas, making it difficult for commanders to manage contractors effectively."[145]

Generally speaking, the record of contract management for intelligence support to contingency operations has been poor. While intelligence organizations have aggressively exploited a wide range of commercial augmentation, they have not dedicated sufficient resources to effectively develop and manage these contracts. Significant shortfalls have occurred in several key aspects of the management process, as noted below.

---

[143] Department of Defense, Office of the Inspector General, *Contracts Awarded for the Coalition Provisional Authority by the Defense Contracting Command - Washington,* Report No. D-2004-057 (18 March 2004): 28, URL: *<http://www.globalsecurity.org/military/library/report/2004/04057sum.htm>*, accessed 30 September 2004.

[144] Government Accountability Office, *Interagency Contracting: Problems with DoD's and Interior's Orders to Support Military Operations,* GAO-05-201 (April 2005), URL: *<http://www.gao.gov/highlights/d05201high.pdf>*, accessed 11 May 2005.

[145] GAO, *Military Operations: Contractors Provide Vital Services to Deployed Forces but are Not Adequately Addressed in DOD Plans,* 3.

THE CONTRACT AWARD PROCESS

The most critical element of any successful program of commercial augmentation is the establishment of effective contract management procedures beginning with the award process. This includes the tasks of identifying requirements, solicitation and circulating requests for proposals, market research and developing contract language. Shortfalls in any step of the development process can make management and surveillance of contract performance difficult, if not impossible, to achieve.

The enormous demands for intelligence support since 9/11 have placed IC organizations under significant pressure to rapidly expand their collection and analytical capabilities. In the rush to provide critical support for contingency operations, there has been significant modification of the acquisition procedures used for many intelligence-related contracts. Several recent government investigations have noted the use of expedited awards procedures that have fallen outside the guidelines established by Federal Acquisition Regulation. This problem was cited as a contributing factor in the Department of the Interior Inspector General report on intelligence support contracts for both Iraq and the detention facility at Guantanamo Bay.[146] These support contracts included commercial augmentation for human intelligence teams, linguistic support, strategic debriefing services, and interrogation support.

Among the issues cited in a recent Department of Interior IG report was the misuse of Blanket Purchase Agreements (BPA) under the GSA schedule to expedite contract awards and bypass an open bidding process.[147] This episode arose as contracting officials misused the GSA schedule labor categories to acquire out-of-scope services for intelligence support activities.[148] For example, the GSA schedule used to procure strategic debriefers, interrogators, counterintelligence agents, and analysts for work in Iraq was classified for "engineering" and "information technology services." A recent GAO review of these contract awards found that "the labor category descriptions in the GSA contracts were, in most cases, significantly different from the descriptions on DoD's statements of work and do not accurately represent the work the contractor performed."[149]

---

[146] Department of Interior, Office of the Inspector General, *Review of 12 Procurements Placed Under General Services Administration Federal Supply Schedules 70 and 871 by the National Business Center*, 16 July 2004 (Washington, DC: DOI Publication, 16 July 2004), 1-5.

[147] Generally speaking, Blanket Purchase Agreements (BPAs) are a simplified contracting vehicle whereby an agency uses an indefinite delivery order for a broad class of goods where the precise quantity and delivery requirements are not known in advance. This contract vehicle is particularly useful for the repeated procurement of individual services over a given period of time. This simplified procurement process is particularly effective for habitual government service providers who offer a known price advantage and have an established performance record.

[148] For a general description of the procedures for GSA Federal Supply Schedule contracts see FAR 38.101. "The Federal Supply Schedule program, pursuant to 41 U.S.C. 259(b)(3)(A), provides Federal agencies with a simplified process of acquiring commercial supplies and services in varying quantities while obtaining volume discounts. Indefinite-delivery contracts are awarded using competitive procedures to firms."

[149] *Interagency Contracting: Problems with DoD's and Interior's Orders to Support Military Operations*, 8. The General Services Administration also awarded similar contracts for interrogation services at Guantanamo Bay detention facility on behalf of the U.S. Army Southern Command. These contracts were canceled in February 2004 when the improper use of the GSA schedule was revealed. Shane Harris, "GSA Canceled Guantanamo Interrogator Contract," GOVEXEC.com. online ed., 16 July 2004, URL: < http://www.govexec.com/dailyfed/0704/071604h1.htm>, accessed 9 May 2005.

In addition to the misapplication of GSA schedules, the IG report also determined that the contracts covering several intelligence-related services in Iraq and Guantanamo Bay lacked sufficient market research and solicitation procedures. According to the IG report, these contracts did not have "an effective system of policies, procedures, and process controls to ensure an equitable and competitive contracting environment that complies with acquisition laws and regulations and protects the public interest."[150] A separate government investigation into the abuse incidents at Abu Ghraib also cited the misuse of the GSA Federal Supply Schedule and added that such "contracts should be carefully scrutinized given the complexity and sensitivity connected to interrogation operations."[151]

Generally speaking, the GSA supply schedule process has many advantages for acquiring routine services from well-established markets. This system can greatly expedite the process of solicitation and market research. The major problems with these contracting vehicles arise because with the GSA system the government loses a significant degree of oversight into how vendors may fulfill an individual task order. The use of the GSA supply schedule generally limits the government's discretion over a vendor's screening and vetting of personnel. Additionally, GSA procedures provide little visibility into how a prime contractor may subcontract out various parts of the required services. Given such limitations on government overview of how such task orders are filled, the use of GSA schedules for sensitive intelligence services should be carefully scrutinized and monitored.

Inappropriately expedited awards also led to other discrepancies in the acquisition process for many support contracts with the Coalition Provisional Authority in Iraq. A separate DoD Inspector General report identified several problems with vague requirements language, improper use of personal services contracts, and the lack of price reasonableness determinations prior to award.[152] Additionally, other procedural irregularities surfaced during investigations of abuse incidents at Abu Ghraib. During the contract development process for interrogation support, the vendor assisted in the drafting of the requirements language and preparation of the Statement of Work (SOW) prior to the contract award. While there are some legal allowances for such collaboration, the subsequent contract award to the same vendor potentially presented a conflict of interest in violation of FAR guidelines.[153]

Many of the cited discrepancies in contracting award procedures may be attributed to the enormous unforeseen operational demands of GWOT operations. This situation placed significant strain on a limited number of contracting officials, many of whom did not possess adequate knowledge of mission requirements or the specific tasks that the vendors would perform. Unfortunately, these shortcomings sometimes resulted

---

[150] Department of Interior Inspector General Report, 3.

[151] AR 15-6 *Investigation of the Abu Ghraib Detention Facility*, 50.

[152] Department of Defense, Office of the Inspector General, *Audit of Contracts Awarded for the Coalition Provisional Authority by the Defense Contracting Command Washington* (18 March 2004) Report No. D-2004-057, URL: <*http://www.globalsecurity.org/military/library/report/2004/04057sum.htm*>, accessed 1 October 2004.

[153] AR 15-6 *Investigation of the Abu Ghraib Detention Facility*, 49.

in the use of questionable contract award procedures. During the initial phases of OEF, numerous deployed intelligence organizations reported critical shortfalls of key personnel, particularly for high-demand intelligence skills involving linguistic and interrogation support. A CENTCOM after-action review of OEF operations reported that "the Army could not provide, and did not have an effective system in place to identify and contract for this support."[154]

DEVELOPING CONTRACT LANGUAGE

Another important shortfall affecting some intelligence service contracting has been the lack of standardized contract language and explicit Statements of Work (SOW). A recent GAO report on DoD contract management procedures observed that generally there is "no standardization of necessary contract language for deployment of contractors."[155] These problems have led to contractor personnel arriving at duty locations with insufficient training, equipment, or professional qualifications for their assigned tasks. In some cases this problem is compounded by the fact that task orders lack precise language describing the nature of services to be performed and the conditions of the work environment. One official involved with OIF contracting commented that "the demands that we asked of our contractors were not always written in the contracts that they were supporting."[156]

---

[154] OPERATION ENDURING FREEDOM: CAAT Initial Impressions Report, 54.

[155] *Military Operations: Contractors Provide Vital Services to Deployed Forces but are Not Adequately Addressed in DOD Plans,* 3.

[156] Roxana Tiron, "Army not Equipped to Manage Contractors on the Battlefield," *National Defense* 88, no. 598 (September 2003), 32.

Outsourcing Signals Intelligence — Can The U.S. Army Do It?[157]

In *How Can the U.S. Army Effectively Outsource Tactical EW/SIGINT to Retain Mission Effectiveness?* Raymond Younger examines whether the Army can or cannot feasibly allow contracting of EW/SIGINT collection and analysis to private industry.

The research addressed the author's concern that outsourcing could have a detrimental effect on mission readiness. The Army intelligence modernization effort attempts to address the proliferation of technology including, for example, the rapid use of spread spectrum communications means. The Army's prescription for future EW/SIGINT capabilities centers on new systems and organizations.

Most importantly for acquisition, Younger analyzes the pitfalls and advantages that outsourcing will have, pointing out private industry and Army considerations, weighing the effects of training, and describing how the Army can benefit from private industry without giving up capabilities. He then examines outsource opportunities and how private industry can complement the current Army SIGINT architecture.

This issue of inadequate SOW language was cited as a compounding factor with contract interrogators serving in OIF. Particularly for sensitive intelligence functions, the report noted that "requiring activities must carefully develop the applicable SOW to include technical requirements and requisite personnel qualifications, experience, and training."[158] The Statement of Work for contract interrogation services used during OIF described a similar skill-set as military occupational specialty 97E, Human Intelligence Collector. Yet many of the contractor personnel were later determined to lack equivalent professional training possessed by their government and uniformed counterparts. Several of the contractors in question had experience in law enforcement or related civilian functions but lacked specific training in military interrogation techniques, the law of land warfare, Geneva Conventions, and applicable DoD intelligence oversight policy.[159] This was also the case for OEF interrogation contractors operating at Bagram Air Base, Afghanistan where later investigations revealed that two of the four contractors had no prior military intelligence training.

---

[157] Raymond Younger, *How Can the U.S. Army Effectively Outsource Tactical EW/SIGINT to Retain Mission Effectiveness?*, (Washington, DC: Joint Military Intelligence College, 2002).

[158] AR 15-6 *Investigation of the Abu Ghraib Detention Facility*, 49.

[159] Department of the Army, "Detainee Operations Inspection" (21 July 2004): 88, URL: <*http://www4. army.mil/ocpa/reports/ArmyIGDetaineeAbuse/*>, accessed 16 August 2004. Legislation now requires that the Secretary of Defense certify that all Federal employees and civilian contractors engaged in the handling or interrogation of detainees must receive training in the laws of war and the Geneva Convention. See U.S. Congress, House, *Ronald W. Reagan National Defense Authorization Act for Fiscal Year 2005*, 108th Cong., 2nd sess., 20 January 2004. H.R. 4200, SEC. 1092 (c). URL: <http://www.wifcon.com/dodauth05.htm>, accessed 11 November 2004.

Part of the difficulty in developing precise SOW language arises from a lack of communication between the contracting authority and the end user of the commercial service. In the case of the OIF interrogation contracts, the SOW did not specify the need for prior training in military interrogation procedures, policy, and doctrine. In some cases the contracting authorities did not possess a background in intelligence operations and therefore lacked familiarity with the specific needs of the receiving unit. These oversights resulted in the deployment of some contract personnel who were not properly screened or qualified for their required duties.

Poorly defined SOW language may also significantly limit the range of labor that a contractor may perform once at their place of duty. On-site Contracting Officer Representatives (COR) are legally unable to revise SOW language based upon changing mission needs without explicit revisions to the contract. Thus, contract personnel will often be pressured by the receiving unit to perform out-of-scope activities for which they are not properly trained or which the contract does not stipulate. In the case of Abu Ghraib, several of the contract personnel performing interrogation and analytical functions were originally employed only for translation services.

Several respondents to this study also noted problems with inflexible contract language limiting the utilization of contract personnel. Often when task orders did not reflect the actual nature of work to be performed on site, there was pressure from the vendor's managers to "grow the contract" outside of the scope of the original proposal. This situation results in operational inefficiencies and unforeseen costs to the government as contracts are modified to reflect the actual conditions of performance.

For sensitive functions such as intelligence collection and analysis it is imperative that Statements of Work, performance standards, and technical qualifications be explicitly defined in the contract language. Effective development of SOW language requires that contracting officers without operational intelligence experience have close interaction with technical experts from the requiring unit and designated on-site CORs, but frequently this does not occur. A GAO report on contract management procedures for several intelligence support contracts in Iraq found that contracting officers "had little to no communication with the CORs in Iraq and did not follow up to obtain monthly reports from them on the contractor's performance....[and] never verified that the Army personnel serving as CORs had appropriate training."[160]

Communication between the contracting officer, the requiring unit, and the designated CORs must begin at the earliest stages of the request for proposal process so that effective market research may be conducted to determine the most suitable vendor, and appropriate contract language developed. Without significant input from the requiring unit and awareness of the mission requirements it is nearly impossible for contracting officers to communicate clear performance expectations to potential vendors. The independent panel reviewing intelligence operations during OIF

---

[160] *Interagency Contracting: Problems with DoD's and Interior's Orders to Support Military Operations*, 12.

concluded that the "continued use of contractors will be required, but contracts must clearly specify the technical requirements and personnel qualifications, experience, and training needed."[161]

MANAGEMENT OF CONTRACT PERSONNEL

One of the major challenges of utilizing commercial augmentation is a lack of understanding of contract management procedures among intelligence leaders. A recent GAO report on army contract management procedures noted that there is generally "inadequate training for staff responsible for overseeing contractors and limited awareness by many field commanders of all contractor activities taking place in their area of operations."[162] A separate report on management procedures for intelligence support in Iraq noted that "the Army officials responsible for overseeing the contractor, for the most part, lacked knowledge of contracting issues and were not aware of their basic duties and responsibilities."[163]

Existing doctrinal guidelines for managing deployed contractors were described in the GAO report as "inconsistent and sometimes incomplete."[164] Even the army's own doctrinal manual for Contractors on the Battlefield acknowledges that "there is no specifically identified force structure nor detailed policy on how to establish contractor management oversight within an AOR. Consolidated contractor management is the goal, but reality is that it has been, and continues to be, accomplished through a rather convoluted system"[165] An independent investigation of OIF interrogation operations reinforced this finding, noting that "oversight of contractor personnel and activities was not sufficient to ensure intelligence operations fell within the law and the authorized chain of command."[166]

Although there is ample doctrinal literature on the generic issue of contract management, there is virtually no guidance specifically dealing with the oversight of commercial intelligence services.[167] The Abu Ghraib investigations revealed that "no doctrine exists to guide interrogators and their intelligence leaders in the contract

---

[161] "Final Report of the Independent Panel to Review DOD Detention Operations," *Independent Panel to Review DOD Detention Operations* (August 2004), 69, URL: <*http://www.defenselink.mil/news/Aug2004/d20040824finalreport.pdf*>, accessed 24 August 2004.

[162] *Military Operations: Contractors Provide Vital Services to Deployed Forces but are Not Adequately Addressed in DOD Plans*, Executive Summary.

[163] *Interagency Contracting: Problems with DoD's and Interior's Orders to Support Military Operations*, 1.

[164] *Military Operations: Contractors Provide Vital Services to Deployed Forces but are Not Adequately Addressed in DOD Plans*, 1.

[165] U.S. Army, Field Manual (FM) 3-100. *Contractors on the Battlefield* (Washington, DC: Department of the Army, January 2003).

[166] "Final Report of the Independent Panel to Review DOD Detention Operations," 69.

[167] The Army's major doctrinal references dealing with contractors in contingency operations are Army Regulation 715-9, Contractors Accompanying the Force; DA Pamphlet 715-16, Contractor Deployment Guide; and Field Manual 3-100.21, Contractors on the Battlefield. These documents are generally geared toward logistics-associated contracting services and offer no guidance on intelligence-specific management or legal issues.

management or command and control of contractors in a wartime environment." Furthermore, the report noted that the "interrogators, analysts, and leaders were unprepared for the arrival of contract interrogators and had no training to fall back on in the management, control and discipline of these personnel."[168] Overall, there was significant confusion among military supervisors over their legal responsibilities for contractor personnel and their ability to dismiss employees for unsatisfactory performance.[169]

The investigations also determined that intelligence "leaders faced numerous issues involving contract management: roles and responsibilities of....personnel with respect to contractors; roles, relationships, and responsibilities of contract linguists and contract interrogators with military personnel; and the methods of disciplining contractor personnel."[170] Clearly, a proximate cause of the failures with OIF detention operations evolved from this lack of familiarity with contract management procedures and confusion over legal responsibilities and control over contract employees.

Based upon respondent feedback for this study, these problems of poor contract management are not uncommon for many intelligence-related augmentation programs. Frequently leaders unfamiliar with their management responsibilities will leave performance evaluation, discipline, and contract oversight to the vendor's on-site manager. In the absence of a government-appointed COR, this approach essentially amounts to the vendors providing their own management and evaluation.

CONTRACTOR TRAINING AND INTEGRATION

Another significant issue of concern with using commercial augmentation for sensitive intelligence operations is proper vetting, training and integration of contract support. Service contracting has several unique challenges that are distinct from engineering or product acquisition where performance specifications can be clearly defined. Performance measures for service contracting are inherently imprecise, but a well-written SOW can clearly articulate the level of training, expertise, and qualifications required of the vendor. Each operational situation is unique and the contracting authority must consider the skills and training that contract personnel may need in order to satisfy all potential mission requirements.

The Department of the Army Inspector General report noted that 35 percent of the contract interrogators at Abu Ghraib lacked any formal training as interrogators. Furthermore, prior to deployment, none of the contractor personnel had received training on Geneva Convention guidelines or the rules of engagement for treatment of detainees.[171] The report found that "the lack of specific training in military policies and techniques has the potential of placing these interrogators [contractors] at a higher

---

[168] AR 15-6 *Investigation of the Abu Ghraib Detention Facility*, 19.

[169] AR 15-6 *Investigation of the Abu Ghraib Detention Facility*, 50.

[170] AR 15-6 *Investigation of the Abu Ghraib Detention Facility*, 18.

[171] AR 15-6 *Investigation of the Abu Ghraib Detention Facility*, 51.

risk of violating Army policies and doctrine, and decreasing intelligence yield."[172] Several respondents in the present study also noted incidents of intelligence support contractors arriving at duty sites with insufficient pre-deployment training, a lack of proper equipment, or inappropriate skill-sets to satisfy mission requirements.

As discussed previously, a significant limitation on the government's power to closely monitor the training and vetting of contractor personnel is the use of the Blanket Purchase Agreement. The Army investigation of Abu Ghraib noted that military supervisors had little or no control over the vetting and pre-training process for arriving contractors. The report found that leaders "knew little of their individual backgrounds or experience and relied on higher headquarters to screen them before arrival. Such screening was not occurring."[173] Several of the contractors were later determined to have little or no experience with intelligence operations, the report noting that the "integration of some contractors without training, qualifications, and certification created ineffective interrogation teams and the potential for non-compliance with doctrine and applicable laws."[174]

Similar problems were also cited in a review of early operations at the detention facility in Guantanamo Bay. Many of the contract linguists supporting the intelligence operations had no experience with military interrogation techniques or intelligence methods. Although contract linguists were screened for basic language proficiency, some of their skills were not appropriately matched for their required duties as interrogators. The original contract SOW listed only generic language requirements but over time the operational demands became more specific as the mission requirements evolved.[175]

Another issue of concern is the deployment of intelligence support contractors. In several cited cases, deployed contractors with interim clearances were unable to serve in their assigned functions while awaiting final clearances, a situation that wasted government resources and created work backlogs for the supported unit. This problem is partly attributable to unmonitored vendors who do not adequately pre-screen their employees and consequently deploy personnel who are later unable to pass the required background checks. In recent years approximately 30-40 percent of linguist candidates provided by DoD vendors never receive final clearance for work on intelligence related missions.[176] Recent rules changes to the DFAR now stipulate that "all required security and background checks be complete and acceptable" prior to deployment.[177] But given the enormous backlog of contractor background investigations, this requirement could

---

[172] "Detainee Operations Inspection," 87.

[173] AR 15-6 *Investigation of the Abu Ghraib Detention Facility,* 40.

[174] AR 15-6 *Investigation of the Abu Ghraib Detention Facility,* 18.

[175] This comment was provided for non-attribution by an intelligence language contract coordinator at the Joint Detention Facility, Guantanamo Bay. Interview and operational questionnaire conducted by author, November 2004.

[176] Lynn McCann, Army Language Support Contracting Officer, Army G2, Intelligence Plans and Operations Directorate, interview by the author, 22 October 2004.

[177] "Defense Federal Acquisition Regulations Supplement; Contractor Personnel Supporting a Force Deployed Outside the United States," 48 CFR Part 252.225-7040 (h).

create an enormous challenge for contracting officers as they try to project support estimates for rapidly changing mission requirements.

In order to effectively utilize commercial augmentation, contracting authorities must have a clear understanding of the operational environment, mission requirements, skills, equipment, clearance, and training requirements of the gaining command. These details must be clearly outlined in the Request for Proposals and articulated in explicit SOW language so that vendors are able to pre-screen the personnel best suited for the requirement. Finally, contract language must clearly provide the government with the power to easily remove and replace any contractor that does not meet the performance expectations established in the SOW.

CONTRACTING OFFICER REPRESENTATIVE TRAINING AND RESPONSIBILITIES

Of the numerous issues that undermine effective contract management, perhaps the biggest challenge is providing quality contract surveillance and performance evaluation. The most frequently cited cause of this shortfall is the lack of properly trained on-site Contracting Officer Representatives (CORs).[178] In many operational scenarios, COR responsibilities are thrust upon intelligence specialists as an "additional duty" to be performed on top of their primary management, analytical, or collection tasks. Many intelligence specialists lack formal training in contract management procedures and are forced to learn through "on the job training." As the Abu Ghraib investigation noted, "if functions such as these [intelligence] are being contracted, MI [military intelligence] personnel need to have at least a basic level of contract training so they can protect the Army's interests."[179] All too often this is not the case. Critical shortages of intelligence personnel have meant that many CORs frequently do not work in close proximity to the site of contract performance and do not have sufficient personnel to effectively assure quality control.

A sampling of several ongoing operational support missions suggests wide variance in the procedures and training for CORs managing intelligence support contracts. During the first 18 months of operations at the joint detention facility in Guantanamo Bay there was no assigned on-site COR monitoring performance under the linguist and interrogation support contracts.[180] Investigations of Abu Ghraib found that "personnel acting as CORs did not, for the most part, have the requisite training and were unaware

---

[178] Training guidelines for CORs vary significantly from command to command. The Defense Federal Acquisition Regulations Supplement is rather vague on precise requirements, stating only that a COR "must be qualified by training and experience commensurate with the responsibilities to be delegated in accordance with department/agency guidelines." *Defense Federal Acquisition Regulations Supplement* (1998): subpart 201.602, URL: <*http://www.acq.osd.mil/dpap/dfars/*>, accessed 27 January 2005.

[179] AR 15-6 *Investigation of the Abu Ghraib Detention Facility*, 51.

[180] This comment was provided for non-attribution by an intelligence language contract coordinator at the Joint Detention Facility, Guantanamo Bay, interview and operational questionnaire conducted by author, November 2004.

of the scope of their duties and responsibilities."[181] Furthermore, there was no dedicated on-site COR monitoring contractor performance at the joint detention facility. The army investigation of detainee abuse incidents specifically noted that "it is very difficult, if not impossible, to effectively administer a contract when the COR is not on site."[182] Fortunately the situation for intelligence support contracts in the Balkans appears to be more closely monitored. Several respondents to this study indicated that multiple CORs were currently tasked to cover intelligence support contracts in the Balkans and all had received appropriate COR training prior to deployment.

An additional challenge for many organizations is that designated CORs will often serve only for short periods of time and are then relocated for operational duties elsewhere. Few intelligence support contracts are afforded dedicated long-term oversight by a single individual. Several respondents contacted for this study also mentioned a lack of good documentation on contract performance; thus, when a new COR arrives on site there is often little evidence of past performance or a sound basis for comparative analysis. Frequent rotations for intelligence personnel only exacerbate this challenge. Commonly the vendor's on-site manager will be the only individual with lengthy operational experience at a given site. All of these factors make it extremely difficult for intelligence specialists without specific contract experience to effectively fulfill their responsibilities as CORs. Ultimately good contract management and on-site surveillance are the only avenues for the government to assure quality of performance as described in the requirements language.

Another challenging aspect of intelligence-related service contracting is defining performance measures and developing effective surveillance methodologies. For many major DoD contracts, dedicated personnel from the Defense Contract Management Agency will oversee vendor performance and evaluation, but these oversight personnel are in short supply. Over the past decade DoD has reduced its acquisition personnel levels by nearly half while during the same time procurement of contract services has more than doubled.[183] As a consequence, for the vast majority of intelligence-related contracts, appointed organizational CORs will serve as the primary monitor. In most cases this COR will be an intelligence specialist rather than a contract specialist; therefore, it is critically important that contract language have clear and measurable performance standards to assist in quantifying vendor performance.

---

[181] *Interagency Contracting: Problems with DoD's and Interior's Orders to Support Military Operations*, 18.

[182] The report observed that "an important step in precluding the reoccurrence of situations where contractor personnel may engage in abuse of prisoner is to ensure that a properly trained COR is on-site. Meaningful contract administration and monitoring will not be possible if a small number of CORs are asked to monitor the performance of one or more contractors who have 100 or more employees in theater, and in some cases, perhaps in several locations." The report concluded that "it is apparent that there was not credible exercise of appropriate oversight of contract performance at Abu Ghraib." AR 15-6 *Investigation of the Abu Ghraib Detention Facility*, 52.

[183] Stephen Barr, "Defense Bills Push for Stricter Contract Procedures," *Washington Post*, online ed., 30 May 2005, URL: < *http://www.washingtonpost.com/wp-dyn/content/article/2005/05/29/AR2005052900991. html*>, accessed 4 June 2005.

Perhaps the greatest challenge for monitoring intelligence service contracts is how to properly define useful metrics for evaluation. Several respondents to this study noted that contracts for intelligence and linguistic services often contain initial qualification criteria for contract personnel but typically will not provide any program for skills maintenance, developmental training, or periodic evaluation. Most of the criteria for work evaluation are informal at best, with little consideration given to developmental counseling or performance review. These tasks are generally left to the vendor's on-site contract manager but often without sufficient government surveillance.

The challenge of defining effective evaluation metrics has become even more important as the government moves toward greater use of Performance-Based Service Acquisitions (PBSA). The PBSA contracting methodology focuses more on results-based evaluation rather than specific process description. With PBSA, the requiring activity defines specific performance goals, known as a Statement of Objectives, then provides the vendor significant latitude in developing a work plan to satisfy the government's needs. The benefit of this approach is that the vendor is not bound by a specific SOW description and is free to devise an optimal solution for meeting the government's needs. DoD established a goal to award 50 percent of all acquisition dollars utilizing PBSA methodology by FY 2005.[184]

Most of the current intelligence-related contracts reviewed for this study still employ traditional SOW methodology in which specific labor functions are clearly defined for the vendor. It is uncertain how the PBSA will be employed for intelligence services as the government moves toward greater use of this contracting methodology. Although PBSA has clear advantages by leveraging vendor expertise to develop creative solutions, this system also places a much greater burden on contracting officers to clearly define the mission objectives, conduct careful market research for appropriate vendors, closely manage performance, and evaluate standards of work and achievement of mission objectives. PBSA only increases the necessity for well-trained on-site intelligence professionals to closely monitor and evaluate the contractor's contribution to overall mission goals. Present deficiencies in contract surveillance practices leave considerable doubt as to the government's ability to adequately utilize these management concepts for sensitive intelligence related missions. Indeed, there are currently significant shortages of government contract officers trained in performance-based acquisition policy.[185] Furthermore, the proper evaluation of performance for these contract vehicles places an even greater burden on the many untrained CORs who are likely to be unfamiliar with PBSA methodologies.

---

[184] Claude M. Bolton, Assistant Secretary of the Army for Acquisition, Logistics and Technology. "Performance Based Service Acquisition," Department of the Army Memorandum, 10 March 2004.

[185] Zack Phillips. "Performance-Based Contracts Gaining Popularity - but is the Government Ready to Use Them?" *CQ.com Homeland Security,* 17 November 2004. URL:<*http://www.cqhls.com/hs/dislay. do?dockey=/cqonline/prod/data/docs/html/hsnews/108*>. Accessed 17 March 2005.

OTHER ISSUES OF CONCERN

Aside from the cited deficiencies in contracting methodology and surveillance measures, several other intangibles must be considered as the government expands its use of commercial augmentation for intelligence functions. Issues of concern that have not been adequately addressed by intelligence policymakers are the long-term cost effectiveness of commercial augmentation, effects of labor competition on government retention, operational flexibility of private sector providers, and equity considerations for government employees working with commercial partners.

The question of whether commercial augmentation is actually a cost-effective long-term management strategy for the government remains unresolved. A quantitative cost-benefit analysis is beyond the scope of this study, but numerous respondents noted that contract personnel are frequently paid several times what their government counterparts make for performing exactly the same intelligence functions. Admittedly, these complaints should be viewed with some skepticism. Short-term contract employees enjoy none of the extensive benefits and job security offered to civil service and military personnel. Furthermore, the vagaries of the marketplace necessitate a certain "risk premium" for contract employees who may be terminated by the government at any time. Additionally, many contract employees possess unique skills, experience, and qualifications that clearly justify differing levels of compensation.

Nevertheless, several respondents mentioned cases of perceived inequities in pay and privilege between contractor and civil service employees, such that some individuals felt a disincentive toward public sector service when they could perform similar functions in the private sector for improved benefits. To some degree, DoD outsourcing policy has exacerbated labor competition and created a "sellers market" for certain high-demand intelligence skills. There is strong indirect evidence suggesting that military and civil service employees already vetted in retirement programs are choosing to leave government service due to the lucrative opportunities in the private sector. This situation has led DoD to implement unprecedented retention bonuses of up to $150,000 for retirement-eligible intelligence specialists under the Critical Skills Retention Bonus Program.[186] This program specifically targets service members serving in the intelligence specialties such as imagery analyst, unmanned aerial vehicle operator, HUMINT collector, and Arabic voice-intercept specialists.

Several respondents to the present study also expressed concern over organizational cohesion and morale due to equity disputes between contractors and government employees working on various intelligence missions. Some respondents expressed the perception that contract workers lacked equivalent dedication to mission accomplishment as their government counterparts. One respondent mentioned a scenario in which several contractors, also military intelligence reservists, were using their deployed status as contractors to "hide" from activation with their respective

---

[186] This program was first introduced in 2002 to retain critical special operations personnel needed for GWOT operations. A recent expansion of this program was announced in January 2005. Jim Tice, "Critical-skills Bonus Program Expanding," *ArmyTimes.com,* 7 March 2005, URL: <*http://www.armytimes.com/ sgmlparse.php?f=archive2/20050307/atpc19257836.sgml*>, accessed 10 March 2005.

reserve units. There is no easy way to ascertain the accuracy of these charges or to quantify the overall impact of such negative perceptions, but these factors must be taken into account if the government is to continue a strategy of substantial commercial augmentation of intelligence support services.

APPLYING THE EVALUATIVE CRITERIA

As these findings suggest, present commercial augmentation programs for intelligence support to GWOT operations are far from optimized. The use of commercial augmentation has been applied primarily as a stop-gap measure to mitigate a significant crisis in intelligence manpower. This situation has led to improper solicitation procedures, poor market research and ineffective contract management. In some cases, contracting practices have skirted the intent of the Federal Acquisition Regulation and lacked sufficient oversight and accountability. Ineffective surveillance plans and a lack of performance metrics have made contract surveillance and evaluation extremely difficult. This mixed record of performance demonstrates serious shortfalls in several key areas of the evaluative criteria.

Of all the difficulties with current commercial augmentation programs for intelligence support, the most troubling aspect is the government's poor record of contract surveillance. Too frequently this important task has been left to untrained personnel, unaware of their responsibilities or simply too far removed from the activities to provide adequate management and control. CORs lack standardized training and the resources necessary to perform their jobs and frequently lack clear metrics to evaluate vendor performance. Compounding this situation, deployed intelligence officers, already heavily burdened with command or analytical responsibilities, are frequently assigned contract management responsibilities as "additional duties." These tasks are not viewed as a core competency among intelligence professionals, and thus are inevitably neglected or simply misunderstood. Due to this generally poor record of contract management, many of the benefits of commercial augmentation are ultimately lost.

THE FUTURE OF COMMERCIALIZED INTELLIGENCE AUGMENTATION

The enormous intelligence demands of the Global War on Terrorism have forced the government into an unanticipated reliance on commercial augmentation. This situation has exposed significant flaws in DoD's contract management methodology. Nevertheless, these short-term challenges should not be used as an excuse to dismiss entirely the potential benefits of commercial augmentation. The lessons of 9/11 and recent counterterrorism operations have demonstrated the inherent weakness of the traditional intelligence bureaucracy. As intelligence reform advocates have noted, the IC organization is "characterized by centralized planning, routinized operations, and a hierarchical chain of command. All of these features leave the intelligence organization ill-suited for the information age."[187]

Traditional bureaucratic structures produce the positive benefits of standardization, predictability, and accountability, but often at the expense of flexibility, innovation, and responsiveness. To succeed against current security challenges, intelligence organizations will need a healthy dose of each quality, enhancing the capabilities of government organizations by leveraging the best talent and technology of the private sector.

Emerging security threats will require that intelligence organizations operate more like private sector entities and less like traditional bureaucracies. Some of this reform will be achieved by adopting the best management practices of successful corporate entities but also by exploiting the enormous potential of well-managed public-private partnerships to create a dynamic synergy of governmental and commercial talent. The challenge for Intelligence Community leaders will be to develop effective procedures for integrating commercial services and establishing safeguards to protect government interests while maximizing the potential benefits of private sector augmentation.

CONSIDERATIONS FOR REFORM

This study concludes with three proposed models for future use of non-governmental resources to augment intelligence collection and analysis. These broadly outlined plans represent a range of policies designed to build a foundation for a dynamic IC surge capacity. The intent of each option is to infuse greater flexibility into the IC talent pool and provide formalized mechanisms to rapidly integrate unique and specialized commercial tools, talent, and technology to satisfy an unpredictable range of operational needs. These proposals offer management strategies that will institutionalize the use of non-governmental resources to enhance the flexibility and effectiveness of the intelligence bureaucracy.

---

[187] Bruce Berkowitz and Allan Goodman, *Best Truth: Intelligence in the Information Age,* New Haven, CT: Yale University Press, 2000, 67.

Option One: A Conservative Approach to Modification of Personnel Hiring Regulations and the Creation of an Intelligence Community Reserve Corps

Among many policymakers within the Intelligence Community there remains significant apprehension with the wholesale privatization of intelligence functions. Some observers cite concern with private corporations gaining too much influence over national security matters. Other critics suggest legitimate fears that privacy rights and civil liberties will be compromised as commercial entities gain greater purview over sensitive personal information or technical collection capabilities. Others argue that excessive privatization efforts will undermine the civil service system and jeopardize the status of government employees. All of these concerns raise valid points and should be considered in any commercial augmentation program.

Notwithstanding these concerns, there remain several management options that support a conservative approach to diversifying the talent and capabilities of the Intelligence Community while still providing greater flexibility for surged operations. As the recent Presidential Commission Report on WMD Intelligence noted, the IC must think more creatively and strategically about tapping external resources, "recognizing that the Community may simply not be the natural home for real expertise on certain topics."[188]

One recent initiative is the National Security Personnel System.[189] This DoD program offers a modified human resources management system permitting the flexible hiring of "highly qualified experts from outside the civil service and uniformed services," exempt from the civil service restrictions established by U.S. Code Title 5.[190] This exemption permits up to 5-year appointments with modified compensation tables to hire individuals "possessing uncommon, special knowledge or skills in a particular occupational field beyond the usual range of expertise" generally available within the Department but needed to satisfy short-term, non-permanent requirements.[191] Although the current DoD program is capped at 2,500 personnel, it does provide a model for the short-term acquisition of unique talents from outside the traditional IC bureaucracy. If successful, this initiative could represent an important tool for the IC to tap resources from industry, academia, and non-governmental organizations to satisfy unanticipated short-term needs for surged collection.

Besides the National Security Personnel System, there are several other models that would permit the IC to better exploit external resources for a more dynamic surge capacity. A 1998 Army War College study suggested a "Civilian Intelligence

---

[188] Commission on the Intelligence Capabilities of the United States Regarding Weapons of Mass Destruction, 2005. URL: <*http://www.state.gov/t/np/rls/fs/29153.htm*>, accessed 15 March 2005.

[189] David S.C. Chu, Under Secretary of Defense for Personnel and Readiness, "Employment of Highly Qualified Experts." 27 February 2004, URL: <*http://www.cpms.osd.mil/fas/staffing/pdf/hqepolicy.pdf*>, accessed 10 May 2005.

[190] "Employment of Highly Qualified Experts," 3.

[191] "Employment of Highly Qualified Experts," 3.

Reserve" program.[192] This proposal envisioned a four-tiered intelligence reserve force for surged contingency operations. Tier One is similar to the current military reserve system with a cadre of former intelligence professionals on-call for organizational augmentation. Tier Two incorporates private U.S. citizens who are not intelligence specialists but vetted professionals with unique expertise in technical matters such as science, finance, or engineering. Tier Three would draw individuals from the private sector to work short-term contracts for more routine Community projects such as program analysis, budget, or administrative tasks. These individuals would be hired in a non-career employment status but in a fashion more formalized than under current commercial augmentation programs. A final tier would comprise private sector and academic specialists who would maintain routine relationships with the IC for long-term analytical projects such as regional indications and warning, in-depth country studies, or specialized technical projects.

A civilian intelligence reserve program offers a reasonable, if not conservative, approach for integrating non-governmental resources into an IC surge capacity. Yet even with this relatively modest proposal there are several potential obstacles such as security and legal oversight concerns, rapid integration of personnel in time of crisis, bureaucratic resistance to outsourcing certain intelligence functions, and the likely reluctance of many private sector and academic professionals to work with the Intelligence Community. Despite these potential shortcomings, a civilian intelligence reserve program is a promising compromise between the bureaucratic status quo and full-scale commercialization.[193]

Another potential model worth consideration is the current DoD feasibility study for the United States Civilian Linguist Reserve Corps (CLRC).[194] The primary objective of the CLRC is to "warehouse high-level expertise in languages that are currently or potentially critical to national security."[195] The proposal identified 47 languages of interest that were operationally relevant to national security, but "where encumbering full-time federal positions is neither practical nor cost-effective." The study recommended that the CLRC "draw from a wide range of civilian expertise both within and outside the federal sector including higher education, non-profit, corporate,

---

[192] Eileen G. Swicker, *Strategic Restructuring of the US Intelligence Community: A Civilian Intelligence Reserve* (Carlisle, PA: U.S. Army War College Strategy Research Project, 1998), URL: <*http://handle.dtic. mil/100.2/ADA342156*>, accessed 4 June 2005.

[193] It should be noted that the Intelligence Reform and Terrorism Prevention Act of 2004 provides the new Director of National Intelligence (DNI) with the authority to experiment with such initiatives. Section 1053 of the legislation outlines a "National Intelligence Reserve Corps" for "the temporary reemployment on a voluntary basis of former employees of elements of the Intelligence Community during periods of emergency." This proposal would include any individual who previously served as a full-time employee within the Intelligence Community. U.S. Congress, House. *Intelligence Reform and Terrorism Prevention Act of 2004*. 108th Cong., 2d sess., 7 December 2004, URL: <*http://www.c-span.org/pdf/s2845confrept. pdf*>, accessed 7 March 2005.

[194] This feasibility study was ordered by the Secretary of Defense as part of the FY 2003 Intelligence Authorization Act, National Defense University, National Security Education Program. *United States Civilian Linguist Reserve Corps Feasibility Study*, 2004, URL: <*http://www.ndu.edu/nsep*>, accessed 12 August 2004.

[195] *United States Civilian Linguist Reserve Corps Feasibility Study*, 8.

and heritage language community sectors... [and] non-traditional sources of expertise for the national security community."[196] This study recommended administration, recruiting, vetting, training, and management of the CLRC be assumed by a quasi-federal government agency or private contractor.

The CLRC concept supports several recent operational recommendations based upon critical language shortfalls identified during GWOT operations. A key finding from after-action reviews of intelligence operations during OEF recommended "establishing a pool of linguists, already granted security clearances and proficient in the diversity of languages needed for short-notice contingencies. Similar to contracting in peacetime and paying a retainer fee to commercial airlines for their support in the war [OEF], the army should identify and begin a formal relationship with native linguists across the United States."[197]

A variation of this program appeared in the January 2005 Defense Language Transformation Roadmap. This DoD proposal would formalize the critical language surge capacity through the use of privately contracted support and standardizing language contract management among all DoD elements under the control of a single executive agent.[198] This proposed management structure would establish common guidelines for counterintelligence procedures, contractor security screenings, bidding and labor pricing, and centralized prioritization of community requirements. Such a program could potentially resolve many shortfalls of the language and intelligence support contracting program experienced during recent operations.

For the most part these proposals fall short of a true privatization program but they do offer a useful, though conservative, approach to establishing a formalized IC surge capacity. These proposals achieve the important goal of infusing greater organizational flexibility into the IC talent pool without significantly jeopardizing the basic bureaucratic structure of the Community. They offer a modest capacity for rapid diversification of the analytical base without raising the significant challenges associated with the management and oversight of extensive commercial augmentation. This conservative approach offers improved operational flexibility while still retaining the accountability, predictability, and standardization of the traditional bureaucratic model.

Option Two: Incremental Reform in Commercial Integration and Contract Management as Core Competency

A more ambitious model for reform takes into account the already extensive use of commercial augmentation and seeks to normalize this approach by strengthening contract management procedures and improving the integration of private sector

---

[196] *United States Civilian Linguist Reserve Corps Feasibility Study,* 5.

[197] U.S. Army Central Command, Combined Arms Assessment Team, "OPERATION ENDURING FREEDOM: CAAT Initial Impressions Report," September 2002.

[198] Department of Defense, *Defense Language Transformation Roadmap,* Washington, DC: GPO, January 2005, 1-15.

resources. As this study has clearly articulated, there are numerous potential benefits of commercial augmentation but current contract administration procedures within the IC are woefully inadequate. In order for the Intelligence Community to reap the full benefits of commercial augmentation, contract management must become a core competency. This complex task cannot be delegated to untrained managers who are overwhelmed with demanding leadership or analytical responsibilities. Contract management cannot become just another "additional duty" for busy intelligence professionals.

In order for a robust program of commercial augmentation to be effective, IC leaders must adopt improved business practices and better management techniques. The effective exploitation of commercial augmentation requires three basic elements.[199] First is the development of a clear business strategy outlining specific mission goals, required skills and services, defined performance standards, and a routinized contract development process. Second is the identification of capable vendors able to provide suitable services and resources to satisfy mission goals. The third, and perhaps most challenging task, is a comprehensive program of contract administration and quality surveillance led by specialists trained in procurement policy and knowledgeable of intelligence operations. These major elements are addressed by the evaluative framework suggested in this paper and reflect the minimum baseline requirements for any successful commercial augmentation program.

These goals are by no means unattainable but they will require the dedicated attention of leaders at the highest level of the Intelligence Community. Such reforms could begin with intelligence organizations adopting the best practices and procedures of the logistical community where there is a generally more well-developed doctrinal approach to contract management. Existing contracting regulations such as the DFAR should be adapted to the unique requirements of intelligence operations and reflect the added challenges of monitoring service-type contracts.

Additionally, contracting officers must become better educated on IC mission requirements and receive improved technical support from intelligence professionals during the contract development process. One possible solution is to encourage an intelligence specialization at the Defense Contract Management Agency (DCMA) where acquisition experts are provided with professionalization opportunities within the Intelligence Community educational system. DCMA contract specialists might potentially attend continuing education programs at intelligence officer advanced schools or participate in programs offered at the Joint Military Intelligence College. After completing this educational immersion, these intelligence contract specialists would be assigned permanent duties at DIA or the J2 specifically to oversee intelligence-related contract management issues. Additionally, these contracting officers must develop a solid knowledge of industry providers and a resource listing of qualified vendors.

---

[199] For an excellent discussion of the contract management process, see Steven Kelman, "Strategic Contracting Management," in *Market-Based Governance: Supply Side, Demand Side, Upside, and Downside,* eds. John D. Donahue and Joseph S. Nye, Washington DC: Brookings Institution Press, 2002.

In order for improved surveillance of contract performance, IC leaders must also make a dedicated effort to properly train Contracting Officer Representatives (CORs) and provide them the tools and resources for effective management. Realistically, intelligence contract management will never become a prestige assignment for IC professionals, but at the very least these individuals must be trained and provided with clear surveillance plans and performance metrics to evaluate vendor service. Outside contract administration, such as from the Defense Contracting Command, has generally not been sufficient to meet IC needs due to manpower shortages and a lack of expertise with IC mission requirements. Given the unique demands of intelligence operations, good management practices will be best achieved if maintained as an internal function within Community organizations.

A final recommendation calls for the establishment of a centralized contracting authority for all IC-related missions. Typically, centralization proposals are greeted with great skepticism among Intelligence Community experts, but the current system of decentralized contracting authority, managed by non-intelligence specialists, has not produced satisfactory results. Under current practice, IC leaders have extremely limited oversight of the myriad commercial suppliers who support the Community as a whole. A more rationalized model might resemble an NGA-like acquisitions directorate establishing a centralized authority for procurement and management of all commercial providers.[200] This consolidated "clearinghouse" approach would provide greater standardization of procurement processes, improved accountability and oversight, as well as more efficient mechanisms for market research, cost comparisons, and evaluation of performance metrics among vendors. A recent IC reform proposal by Sen. Saxby Chambliss (D-GA) has called for the consolidation of the entire military intelligence community under an "INTCOM" unified command structure.[201] If such a proposal were adopted it would be the logical embryo for a unified intelligence contracting command that would greatly strengthen management and oversight of commercial augmentation programs.

These reform proposals offer the baseline requirements needed for the effective management, integration, and oversight of commercial intelligence augmentation. With improved controls and management procedures it is possible to imagine a much wider range of future applications for commercialized intelligence support, particularly as private sector providers establish strong records of accountability and performance. Some observers have gone so far as to suggest that the IC should actively seek to "off-load" certain operational responsibilities as soon as commercial entities are capable of handling them, noting that "if intelligence consumers could use a commercial substitute whenever they found one that met their needs, intelligence managers would have more opportunity (and incentive) to concentrate on those highly specialized areas in which government has a comparative advantage."[202]

---

[200] For a brief description of the role of NGA's Acquisitions Directorate, see URL: <*http://www.nga. mil/portal/site/nga01/index.jsp?epicontent=GENERIC&itemID=46c86591e1b3af00VgnVCMServer23727 a95RCRD&beanID=1629630080&viewID=Article*>.

[201] Senator Chambliss intends to reintroduce legislation for a unified intelligence command during the 109th Congress. Saxby Chambliss, "We Have Not Correctly Framed the Debate on Intelligence Reform," *Parameters* 35, no. 1 (Spring 2005), 5-13.

[202] *Best Truth: Intelligence in the Information Age,* 46.

The potential scenarios for such a capability are easily imaginable. Routine surveillance duties or monitoring of demilitarized zones such as the Sinai or the Balkans could be adequately managed by properly equipped commercial enterprises. Intelligence support to United Nations missions or to non-governmental humanitarian relief efforts are other scenarios where specialized private sector corporations could provide surveillance functions, open-source collection, and mission-focused analysis. The integration of private corporations into these lower-priority missions could potentially free operational forces to concentrate on more difficult higher-priority contingency operations.

Option Three: Radical Change into A Virtual Networked Intelligence Community

The final proposal is a step beyond what current augmentation programs provide. It offers an aggressive model for market-based governance that challenges the basic structure of the intelligence bureaucracy, replacing it with a "networked" organizational model that is highly responsive, adaptable, innovative, and scalable.[203] Rather than simply consuming the products of commercialization, the IC would re-craft itself along a corporate model and become a strategic competitor for the best talent and technology in the private sector. As several IC reform advocates have observed, "the Intelligence Community needs at least as much flexibility as private corporations. Many of its requirements for specialized information are likely to change quickly. Traditional civil service tenure is probably suited only for employees with the most general, long-term skills."[204] As one study of intelligence privatization has suggested the "strength of non-governmental intelligence is partially based upon its high degree of operational flexibility, a minimal need to acquiesce to political constituencies, a higher level of efficiency and often, a better return on investment."[205] The value of market-based governance models would permit IC organizations to capitalize on these inherent qualities of private sector enterprise.

The concept of networked governance is a somewhat ambiguous term but it has been used to describe a process whereby state agencies rely upon the collaboration of a variety of non-governmental providers to deliver a public good. The most attractive feature of this model is its enormous potential for dynamic collaboration as traditional bureaucracy is replaced by a consortium of independent providers. In essence, this has been the model for defense hardware procurement for some time — a directed partnership among strategic planners, government research and development programs, independent think tanks, and private industry.

The proposed system would create a dynamic, networked, virtual intelligence program based upon the model of the Defense Advanced Research Projects Agency's

---

[203] For a general discussion of the concept of "networked government," see Elaine Ciulla Kamarck, "The End of Government as We Know It," in *Market-Based Governance: Supply Side, Demand Side, Upside, and Downside*, eds. John D. Donahue and Joseph S. Nye, Washington DC: Brookings Institution Press, 2002.

[204] *Best Truth: Intelligence in the Information Age*, 56.

[205] James R. Sutton, *Subversion of a Government Monopoly: The Privatization of Intelligence Services* (Erie, PA: Research Intelligence Consortium, Inc, February 2000), 7.

management structure.[206] As an agency focused on "revolutionary, high-payoff research," DARPA's management model minimizes facilities, institutional structures, and permanent personnel. As a key element of this management philosophy, "DARPA invests about 90 percent of its funds at organizations outside of federal government, primarily at universities and in industry."[207] The organizational goal is to build dynamic, innovative, short-term project management teams to solve DoD's most difficult technical problems.

Of particular relevance to this study is DARPA's use of several special contracting authorities to build its project teams. The use of "Experimental Personnel Authority" provides DARPA with significant latitude to acquire unique technical expertise and develop contractual relationships with the private sector entities and research universities. These authorities permit the Secretary of Defense to carry out programs under a special personnel management authority to hire temporary "employees in the civil service, appoint scientists and engineers from outside the civil service and uniformed services...without regard to any provision of title 5, United States Code."[208] These short-term, project-based management teams are able to avoid the formation of institutional interests that inhibit innovation and discourage collaboration with non-governmental expertise.

Certainly a DARPA-like program of "networked government" is not suitable or necessary for many routine intelligence functions, but it does offer a potential model for managing short-term surge requirements and providing an innovative structure for conducting the type of serious in-depth research that is often sacrificed to the daily demand for current intelligence products. Among the recommendations of the committee report on WMD intelligence failures was the creation of a not-for-profit "sponsored research institution" to serve the Intelligence Community. Such an organization would be financed by IC dollars but insulated from Community management in order to seek innovative and creative solutions to the nation's most demanding technical and analytical challenges. Although this type of virtual networked community is not suitable for most Intelligence Community organizations, the approach does offer a model for using the government's contracting power to develop focused, adaptable, and specialized teams to tackle a broad range of intelligence challenges that are not met by the traditional bureaucratic structure.

---

[206] For a general overview of DARPA's management and contracting philosophy, see Defense Advanced Research Projects Agency, *Bridging the Gap: DARPA Overview*, March 2004, URL: *<http://www.darpa. mil/body/pdf/BridgingTheGap_Feb_05.pdf>*, accessed 21 January 2004.

[207] *Bridging the Gap: DARPA Overview*, 8.

[208] 5 U.S.C. § 3104. "Experimental Personnel Program for Scientific and Technical Personnel."

Are There Practical Examples of "Thinking Outside The Box?"[209]

CarolLyn Lewis's *Technology Investment Agreements and the Technology Fellowship: A Case Study for Thinking Outside the Tool Box* presents an example of contracting methods that take the Intelligence Community outside of a comfort zone, into new methods that may be more relevant to changed and radically improved communication and technological skills.

In her research Lewis proposes that a Technology Fellowship Program (TFP) could inject future National Reconnaissance Office (NRO) mission needs into current industry research and development (IR&D) programs, and that one-year research fellowships with experts in a particular technology may benefit NRO long-term objectives. TFP objectives include the participant's solving a research problem during the fellowship, and then taking lessons learned and ideas for supporting government initiatives back to industry. Using a Technical Investment Agreement (TIA) instead of a standard contract vehicle would improve the amount of participation from industry. Though commonly used in federal agencies, sectors of the Intelligence Community have been slow to embrace TIAs, apparently unaware they exist. Recognizing that her proposal will shift the type of participating commercial business away from the traditional consulting firms that held the majority of the fellowships, she is aware of the challenges in an arena that has not readily accepted rapid or radical changes.

---

[209] CarolLyn Lewis, *Technology Investment Agreements and the Technology Fellowship: A Case Study for Thinking Outside the Tool Box,* unpublished MSSI Thesis, Washington, DC: Joint Military Intelligence College, 2004.

CONCLUSION

The three proposed models provide a range of potential options for harnessing non-governmental and commercial resources to create a dynamic, flexible, and responsive IC surge capacity. To varying degrees all three proposals require some basic reconsideration of the traditional IC bureaucracy, but it is important to note that none of the options relieves the government of responsibility for careful contract development, good management practices, and effective surveillance methodologies. Thus, the present study offers the baseline evaluative criteria that must be applied to any program of commercial augmentation.

Regardless of the future direction of IC reform, some form of commercial augmentation will undoubtedly play a vital role in the collection, analysis, and production of intelligence support to national security policy. In order to meet the security challenges of the post-9/11 world, private industry must be viewed as a strategic partner of the Intelligence Community. Collaborative effort with non-governmental entities offers a powerful mechanism to diversify and strengthen the IC's collection and analytical capabilities, but to fully realize the benefit of these resources the management and oversight of commercial providers must become a core competency for all intelligence organizations.

APPENDIX

Evaluative Criteria for Determining the Applicability of Commercialized Intelligence Augumentation: Consolidated Case Study Overview			
Evaluative Criteria	**Personnel Security Investigations**	**Commercial Remote Sensing**	**GWOT Operational Support**
Acceptability of Private Sector Involvement			
Contract service does not perform inherently governmental functions	✓	✓	?
Contract administration adheres to proper solicitation and award procedures	✓	✓	✗
Contract service does not undermine operational security	✗	✗	?
Vendor offers a best value alternative (price and performance standards)	✗	✓	?
Suitability of Vendor Services			
Vendor offer-unique services or products unavailable in the public sector	✓	✓	✓
Vendor offers scalability if service and flexible output to meet mission requirements	✗	✗	✓
Contract is negotiated in a mature market environment with in-sector competition	✓	✗	✗
Bidder offers past performance record and known reliability	✗	✓	?
Accountability of Contract Management Procedures			
Contract language offers clear legal oversight and accountability	✓	✓	✗
Contract offers clear Statement of Work (SOW) and evaluation procedures	✓	✓	✗
Contract provides effective integration plan and clear performance measures	✗	✓	✗
Government possesses sufficiently trained, on-site contract management personnel	✗	✓	✗

BIBLIOGRAPHY

"Abuse by Outsourcing." Editorial. *Washington Post*, online ed., 26 May 2004. URL: *<http://www.washingtonpost.com/wp-dyn/articles/A55980-2004May25.html>*. Accessed 26 May 2004.

Alexander, Keith B., LTG, USA, Army Deputy Chief of Staff for Intelligence. "Memorandum: Contractor Support to Army Counterintelligence," 10 June 2004.

_____. Statement before the Committee on Armed Services Subcommittee on Strategic Forces. 108th Cong., 2d sess., 7 April 2004. URL: *<http://armed-services.senate.gov/statemnt/2004/April/Alexander.pdf>*. Accessed 2 May 2005.

Apgar, Mahlon, and John Keane. "New Business with the New Military." *Harvard Business Review* 82, no. 9 (September 2004): 45-56.

Barr, Stephen. "Defense Bills Push for Stricter Contract Procedures." *Washington Post,* online ed., 30 May 2005. URL: < *http://www.washingtonpost.com/wp-dyn/content/article/2005/05/29/AR2005052900991.html>*. Accessed 4 June 2005.

Berkowitz, Bruce, and Allan Goodman. *Best Truth: Intelligence in the Information Age.* New Haven, CT: Yale University Press, 2000.

Biesecker, Calvin. "OMP Selects Five Contractors to Expand Capacity for Background Checks." *Defense Daily*, online ed., 28 July 2004. URL: *<http://web.lexis-nexis.com/universe/document>*. Accessed 21 September 2004.

Bolton, Claude M., Assistant Secretary of the Army for Acquisition, Logistics and Technology. "Performance Based Service Acquisition." Department of the Army Memorandum, 10 March 2004.

Bowman, Gregory L., MAJ, USA. "Transforming Installation Security: Where Do We Go from Here?" *Military Law Review,* 178, Winter 2003, 50-93.

Brooks, Douglas. "The Business End of Military Intelligence: Private Military Companies." *Military Intelligence Professional Bulletin* (July-September 1999): 42-46. URL: *<http://www.fas.org/irp/agency/army/tradoc/usaic/mipb/1999-3/brooks.htm>*. Accessed 15 August 2004.

Bruner, Edward. "Military Forces: What is the Appropriate Size for the United States?" Washington, DC: Congressional Research Service, May 2004.

Burlas, Joe. "IG: Individual Discipline Failures Led to Detainee Abuse." *Army News Service,* 22 July 2004. URL: *<http://www.au.af.mil/au/awc/awcgate/army/ig_abuse22jul04.htm>*. Accessed 10 August 2004.

Caruso, Brook A. *The Mexican Spy Company: United States Covert Operations in Mexico, 1845-1848.* Jefferson, NC: McFarland and Company Inc., 1991.

Cha, Ariana Eunjung, and Renae Merle. "Line Increasingly Blurred Between Soldiers and Civilian Contractors." *Washington Post,* online ed., 13 May 2004. URL:*<http://www.washingtonpost.com/wp-dyn/articles/A22547-2004May12.html>*. Accessed 13 May 2004.

Chambliss, Saxby. "We Have Not Correctly Framed the Debate on Intelligence Reform." *Parameters 35*, no. 1, Spring 2005, 5-13.

Chu, David S.C., Under Secretary of Defense for Personnel and Readiness. "Employment of Highly Qualified Experts." 27 February 2004. URL: <http://www.cpms.osd.mil/fas/staffing/pdf/hqepolicy.pdf>. Accessed 10 May 2005.

Clapper, James R., Lieutenant General, USAF (Ret.). Director, National Geospatial-Intelligence Agency. Untitled lecture given at the Joint Military Intelligence College, Distinguished Speaker Program. Washington, DC, 5 December 2004. Comments used with permission of the speaker.

Colligan, William, CPT, USA. *The Privatization of Personnel Security: The Effects of the National Performance Review on the Intelligence Community.* Online MSSI Thesis, Washington, DC: Joint Military Intelligence College, 2000.

Cooper, Mary H. "Privatizing the Military." *CQ Researcher* 14, no. 24, 25 June 2004, 568-587.

Commission on the Roles and Capabilities of the U.S. Intelligence Community. *Preparing for the 21st Century: An Appraisal of U.S. Intelligence,* 1996. URL:<http://www.access.gpo.gov/int/report.html>. Accessed 11 August 2004.

Contracting Officer's Representative Course Handbook. Vienna, VA: Management Concepts Incorporated, 2004.

Council on Foreign Relations. *Making Intelligence Smarter: The Future of U.S. Intelligence, Report of an Independent Task Force,* 1996. URL: <http://www.copi.com/articles/intelrpt/cfr.html>. Accessed 10 August 2004.

Dandar, Edward. "Is Outsourcing the Answer?" *INSCOM Journal* 20, no. 2 (1997): 18. URL: <http://www.fas.org/irp/agency/inscom/journal/97-mar-apr/marapr18.htm>. Accessed 10 August 2004.

Defense Advanced Research Projects Agency. *Bridging the Gap: DARPA Overview.* March 2004. URL: <http://www.darpa.mil/body/pdf/BridgingTheGap_Feb_05.pdf>. Accessed 21 January 2004.

Defense Security Service (DSS) Augmentation Programs," Web-only document. URL: <www.dss.mil/aboutdss/augmentation>. Accessed 17 September 2004.

Department of the Army, Office of the Deputy Chief of Staff for Intelligence. *Army Language Master Plan.* Washington, DC: Department of the Army, 3 January 2000.

_____. Office of the Inspector General. AR 15-6 *Investigation of Abu Ghraib Prison and the 205th Military Intelligence Brigade.* Investigating Officer: LTG Anthony R. Jones. URL: <http://www.globalsecurity.org/intell/library/reports/2004/800-mp-bde.htm>. Accessed 25 August 2004.

_____. Office of the Inspector General, *Contracts Awarded for the Coalition Provisional Authority by the Defense Contracting Command — Washington,* Report No. D-2004-057 (18 March 2004): 28. URL: <http://www.globalsecurity.org/military/library/report/2004/04057sum.htm>. Accessed 30 September 2004.

_____. *Detainee Operations Inspection,* 21 July 2004. URL: <http://www4.army.mil/ocpa/reports/ArmyIGDetaineeAbuse>. Accessed 16 August 2004.

Department of Defense. *Defense Federal Acquisition Regulations Supplement* (1998). URL: <http://www.acq.osd.mil/dpap/dfars/>. Accessed 27 January 2005.

_____. *Defense Language Transformation Roadmap.* Washington, DC: GPO, January 2005.

_____. *Handbook for the Preparation of Statement of Work.* Washington, DC: GPO, 1996.

_____. Office of the Inspector General. *Audit of Contracts Awarded for the Coalition Provisional Authority by the Defense Contracting Command Washington,* Report No. D-2004-057, 18 March 2004. URL: *<http://www.globalsecurity.org/military/library/report/2004/04057sum.htm>.* Accessed 1 October 2004.

_____. Office of the Inspector General. S*tatement of Donald Mancuso, Acting Inspector General Department of Defense before the Subcommittee on National Security, Veterans Affairs and International Relations, House Committee on Government Reform on Defense Security Oversight, Report No. D-2000-198,* 20 September 2000. URL: *<http://www.fas.org/sgp/congress/2000/mancuso.html>.* Accessed 10 November 2004.

_____. *Quadrennial Defense Review: America's Security in the 21st Century.* Washington, DC: Government Printing Office, 2001.

Department of Interior, Office of the Inspector General. *Review of 12 Procurements Placed Under General Services Administration Federal Supply Schedules 70 and 871 by the National Business Center.* Washington, DC: DOI Publication, 16 July 2004

Dowling, Thomas E., *Intelligence in the Final Indian Wars, 1866-1887,* MSSI Thesis, Washington, DC: Joint Military Intelligence College, September 1996.

Dunlay, Thomas W. *Wolves for the Blue Soldiers: Indian Scouts and Auxiliaries with the United States Army, 1860-90.* Lincoln: University of Nebraska Press, 1982.

Dycus, Stephen, and others. *National Security Law,* 3rd ed. New York: Aspin Publishers, 2002.

Fay, George R., MG, USA. AR 15-6 *Investigation of the Abu Ghraib Detention Facility and 205th Military Intelligence Brigade*, 2004. URL: *<http://www.globalsecurity.org/intell/library/reports/2004/800-mp-bde.htm>.* Accessed 25 August 2004.

"Final Report of the Independent Panel to Review DOD Detention Operations." *Independent Panel to Review DOD Detention Operations,* August 2004, URL: *<http://www.defenselink.mil/news/Aug2004/d20040824finalreport.pdf>.* Accessed 24 August 2004.

Finley, James P. "Apache Scouts in the Punitive Expedition." *Huachuca Illustrated* 1, 1993, 1-5. URL: *<http://www.lib.byu.edu/~rdh/wwi/comment/huachuca/H11-23.htm>.* Accessed 28 October 2004.

Finnegan, John Patrick. *Army Lineage Series: Military Intelligence.* Washington, DC: Center of Military History, 1998. URL: *<http://www.army.mil/cmh-pg/books/Lineage/mi/mi-fm.html>.* Accessed 21 October 2004.

Fishel, Edwin C. *The Secret War for the Union: The Untold Story of Military Intelligence in the Civil War.* Boston: Houghton Mifflin Company, 1996.

Gansler, Jacques S., Under Secretary of Defense for Acquisition and Technology.

"Guidebook for Performance-Based Services Acquisition (PBSA) in the Department of Defense." 2 January 2001. URL: <*http://www.acq.osd.mil/dpap/Docs/pbsaguide010201.pdf>*, accessed 2 May 2005.

General Services Administration. *Federal Acquisition Regulation,* September 2001. URL: <*http://www.arnet.gov/far/>*. Accessed 6 October 2004.

Gibson, Gail, and Scott Shane. "Contractors Act as Interrogators." *Baltimore Sun,* online ed., 4 May 2004. URL: <*http://www.baltimoresun.com/news/nationworld/bal-te.contractors04may04,0,6476999.story>*. Accessed 10 August 2004.

Goodman, Allan, and others. *In from the Cold: The Report of the Twentieth Century Fund Task Force on the Future of U.S. Intelligence.* New York: The Twentieth Century Fund Press, 1996.

Government Accountability Office. *DoD Needs to Overcome Impediments to Eliminating Backlog and Determining Its Size.* GAO-04-344, February 2004. URL: <*http://www.gao.gov/highlights/d04344high.pdf>*. Accessed 10 November 2004.

_____. *Foreign Languages: Human Capital Approach Needed to Correct Staffing and Proficiency Shortfalls.* GAO-02-375, January 2002. URL: <*http://www.gao.gov/new.items/d02375.pdf>*. Accessed 13 October 2004.

_____. *Inadequate Personnel Security Investigations Pose National Security Risks.* GAO/NSIAD-00-12, October 1999. URL: <*http://www.gao.gov/archive/2000/ns00065t.pdf>*. Accessed 13 November 2004.

_____. *Inadequate Personnel Security Investigations Pose National Security Risks,* Statement of Carol R. Schuster, Associate Director, National Security Preparedness Issues, National Security and International Affairs Division, Testimony before the Subcommittee on National Security, Veterans Affairs, and International Relations. GAO/T-NSIAD-00-65, 16 February 2000. URL: <*http://www.gao.gov/archive/2000/ns00065t.pdf>*. Accessed 9 March 2005.

_____. *Interagency Contracting: Problems with DoD's and Interior's Orders to Support Military Operations.* GAO-05-201, April 2005. URL: <*http://www.gao.gov/highlights/d05201high.pdf>*. Accessed 11 May 2005.

_____. *Intelligence Reform: Human Capital Considerations Critical to 9/11 Commission's Proposed Reforms.* GAO-04-1084T, September 2004. URL: < *http://www.gao.gov/new.items/d041084t.pdf* >. Accessed 13 November 2004.

_____. *Military Operations: Contractors Provide Vital Services to Deployed Forces but Are Not Adequately Addressed in DOD Plans.* GAO-03-695, June 2003. URL: <*http://www.gao.gov/highlights/d03695high.pdf* >. Accessed 13 October 2004.

Grinfeld, Michael J. "War Incorporated." *California Lawyer,* May 2005: 22-28.

Grossman, Elaine M. "Possible Interrogation Contractor Influence Cited in Senate Vote." *Inside the Pentagon,* online edition, 24 June 2004. URL: <*http://www.d-n-i.net/grossman/contractor_influence_cited.htm>*. Accessed 22 October 2004.

Guttman, Dan. "The Shadow Pentagon." *The Center for Public Integrity* (September 2004), online study. URL: <*http://www.publicintegrity.org/pns/report.aspx?aid=386>*. Accessed 30 September 2004.

Harrington, Caitlin. "Backlog of Pentagon Security Clearances Nearing 200,000." *CQ.com Homeland Security,* 26 May 2004. URL: <*http://www.cqhls.com/hs/dislay.do?dockey/cqonline/prod/data/docs/html/hsnews/108*>. Accessed 17 March 2005.

Harris, Shane. "Defense Department Lacks Staff to Tackle Security Clearance Backlog." *GOVEXEC.com.* online ed., 27 May 2004. URL: <*http://www.govexec.com/dailyfed/0504/052704h1.htm*>. Accessed 21 September 2004.

_____. "GSA Canceled Guantanamo Interrogator Contract." *GOVEXEC.com.* online ed., 16 July 2004. URL: <*http://www.govexec.com/dailyfed/0704/071604h1.htm*>. Accessed 9 May 2005.

Henry, Patrick T., Assistant Secretary of the Army. "Intelligence Exemption Memorandum for the Assistant Deputy Chief of Staff for Intelligence," 26 December 2000.

"Interim Rule to the Defense Federal Acquisition Regulation Supplement (DFARS): Personal Services Contracts." *Federal Register* 69, No. 180, 17 September 2004. URL: <*http://www.acq.osd.mil/dpap/dars/dfars/changenotice*>. Accessed 3 November 2004.

Kupchinsky, Roman. "Information Revolution Feeds Alternative Intelligence Market." Radio Free Europe/Radio Liberty, 23 May 2005. URL: <*http://www.rferl.org/featuresarticle/2005/05/e1dc62e7-504a-4abb-a61f-008f7167bfab.html*>. Accessed 3 June 2005.

Lewis, CarolLyn, *Technology Investment Agreements and the Technology Fellowship: A Case Study for Thinking Outside the Tool Box,* unpublished MSSI Thesis, Washington, DC: Joint Military Intelligence College, 2004.

Lowenthal, Mark. "Open Source Intelligence: New Myths, New Realities." *Defense Daily News Special Reports,* 2004. URL: <*http://www.defensedaily.com/reports/osintmyths.htm*>. Accessed 10 August 2004.

Lowenthal, Mark, and Robert David Steele. "Open Source Intelligence: Private Sector Capabilities to Support DOD Policy, Acquisition, and Operations." *Defense Daily News Special Reports,* 2004. URL: <*http://www.fas.org/irp/eprint/oss980501.htm*>. Accessed 10 August 2004.

Makinson, Larry. "Outsourcing the Pentagon." *The Center for Public Integrity,* (September 2004). URL: <*http://www.publicintegrity.org/pns/report.aspx?aid=386*>. Accessed 30 September 2004.

Market-Based Governance: Supply Side, Demand Side, Upside, and Downside. Eds. John D. Donahue and Joseph S. Nye. Washington, DC: Brookings Institution Press, 2002.

McCarthy, Ellen. "Changes behind the Barbed Wire: New Standards are in Place for the Oversight of Contract Workers at Abu Ghraib Prison." *Washington Post,* online ed., 13 December 2004. URL: <*http://www.washingtonpost.com/wp-dyn/articles/A59673-2004Dec12.html*>. Accessed 13 December 2004.

"Measure Banning Private Sector Interrogations Fails in Senate." *GOVEXEC.com Daily Briefing,* online ed. 16 June 2004. URL: <*http://www.govexec.com/dailyfed/0604/061604cdpm4.htm*>. Accessed 22 October 2004.

Mercado, Stephen C. "Sailing the Sea of OSINT in the Information Age," *Studies in Intelligence: Journal of the American Intelligence Professional* 48, no. 3 (2004): 45-55.

National Defense University, National Security Education Program. *United States Civilian Linguist Reserve Corps Feasibility Study,* 2004. URL: *<www.ndu.edu/ nsep>*. Accessed 12 August 2004.

National Security Personnel System, NSPS Design and Implementation, Web-only document. URL: *<http://www.cpms.osd.mil/nsps>*. Accessed 23 November 2004.

Nestercznk, George. "Reviewing the National Performance Review." *Regulation* 19, No. 3, 1996. URL: *<http://www.cato.org/pubs/regulation/reg19n3b.html>*. Accessed 10 November 2004.

"NGA Taps ORBIMAGE for Clearview." *GEO World, Government Connection.* May 2004, URL: *<http://www.geoplace.com/uploads/georeport/040407.htm>*. Accessed 16 November 2004.

Office of Management and Budget. "Federal Acquisition Regulation, Circular No. A-76." 4 August 1983, revised 1999. URL: *<http://www.whitehouse.gov/omb/ circulars/a076/a076.html>*. Accessed 25 August 2004.

O'Harrow, Robert. "In Age of Security, Firm Mines Wealth of Personal Data." *Washington Post,* online ed., 20 January 2005. URL: *<http://www. washingtonpost.com/wp-dyn/articles/A22269-2005Jan19.html>*. Accessed 20 January 2005.

OPERATION IRAQI FREEDOM Study Group. "Intelligence Battlefield Operating System Initial Observations." 19 June 2003. URL: *<https://www.calldr. leavenworth.army.mil>*. Accessed 13 November 2004.

Perlak, Joseph R., MAJ, USA. "The Military Extraterritorial Jurisdiction Act of 2000: Implications for Contractor Personnel." *Military Law Review* 169, September 2001, 93-141.

Phillips, Zack. "Performance-Based Contracts Gaining Popularity—but is the Government Ready to Use Them?" *CQ.com Homeland Security,* 17 November 2004. URL: *<http://www.cqhls.com/hs/dislay.do?dockey=/cqonline/prod/data/ docs/html/hsnews/108>*. Accessed 17 March 2005.

Reddy, Anitha, and Ellen McCarthy. "CACI in the Dark on Reports of Abuse." *Washington Post,* online ed., 6 May 2004. URL: *<http://www.washingtonpost. com/ac2/wp-dyn/A5677-2004May5?language=printer>*. Accessed 6 May 2004.

Regalado, Antonio. "U.S. Allows Dissemination of Satellite Photos of Iraq." *The Wall Street Journal,* 21 March 2003. URL: *<http://www.globalsecurity.org/org/ news/2003/030321-iraq-imagery01.htm>*. Accessed 16 November 2004.

Rose, P.K. *The Founding Fathers of American Intelligence.* Washington DC: CIA, Center for the Study of Intelligence, 1999. URL: *<http://www.cia.gov/csi/ books/940299/art-1.html>*. Accessed 21 October 2004.

Schooner, Steven L. "Contractor Atrocities at Abu Ghraib: Compromised Accountability in a Streamlined, Outsourced Government" *Stanford Law and Policy Review* 16, No. 2, 2005. URL: *<http://papers.ssrn.com/sol3/papers.cfm?abstract_ id=605367>*. Accessed 23 November 2004.

Schwartz, Nelson D., and Noshua Watson. "The Pentagon's Private Army." *Fortune,* 17, March 2003, 100-105.

Shorrock, Tim. "The Spy Who Billed Me." *Mother Jones,* January-February 2005. URL:<*http://www.motherjones.com/news/outfront/2005/01/12_400.html*>. Accessed 8 March 2005.

Sietzen, Frank. "A Clearview of NIMA's Commercial Imagery Use." *Geospatial Solutions,* online ed., 1 March 2003. URL: <*http:www.geospatialonline.com/ geospatialsolutions/content/jps?id=4*>. Accessed 16 September 2004.

Singer, Peter. *Corporate Warriors: The Rise of the Privatized Military Industry.* Ithaca, NY: Cornell University Press, 2003.

_____. "The Contract the Military Needs to Break." *Washington Post,* 12 September 2004, B4.

Smith, Eugene. "The New Condottieri and U.S. Policy: The Privatization of Conflict and Its Implications." *Parameters* 32, no. 4, Winter 2002 – 2003, 104-119.

Smith, Marcia S. *U.S. Space Programs: Civilian, Military, and Commercial.* Washington, DC: Library of Congress, Congressional Research Service, 2003.

Starks, Tim. "ManTech Wins a Seat on Defense Intelligence and Security Contract," *CQ.com Homeland Security,* 25 January 2005. URL: <*http://www.cqhls.com/hs/ display.do?dockey/cqonline/prod/data/docs/html*>. Accessed 17 March 2005

Steele, Robert David. "Relevant Information: A New Approach to Collection, Sharing and Analysis." Unpublished white paper by the OSS Academy, 15 March 1999. URL: <*http://downloads.securityfocus.com/library/infowar/papers/ ISDoctrine.doc*>. Accessed 10 May 2005.

_____. *The New Craft of Intelligence: Personal, Public and Political.* Oakton, Virginia: OSS International Press, 2002. URL: <*http://www.oss.net/dynamaster/ file_archive/020731/7e44d06d4268c8b030d47d58c01fca03/chapter15.doc*>. Accessed 8 August 2004.

Strohecker, Scott J. *Peacekeeping for Hire? The Potential Role of Private Military Companies in Peace Operations,* MSSI Thesis, Washington, DC: Joint Military Intelligence College, 1999.

Sutton, James R. *Subversion of a Government Monopoly: The Privatization of Intelligence Services.* Erie, PA: Research Intelligence Consortium, Inc, February 2000.

Swicker, Eileen G. *Strategic Restructuring of the US Intelligence Community: A Civilian Intelligence Reserve.* Carlisle Barracks, PA: U.S. Army War College Strategy Research Project, 1998. URL: <*http://handle.dtic.mil/100.2/ADA342156*>. Accessed 4 June 2005.

"The Information Edge: Imagery Intelligence and Geospatial Information in an Evolving National Security Environment," *Report of the Independent Commission on the National Imagery and Mapping Agency,* December 2000. URL: <*http://www.fas. org/irp/agency/nima/commission/article02.htm*>. Accessed 16 September 2004.

Tice, Jim. "Critical-skills Bonus Program Expanding." *ArmyTimes.com,* 7 March 2005. URL:<*http://www.armytimes.com/sgmlparse.php?f=archive2/20050307/ atpc19257836.sgml*>. Accessed 10 March 2005.

Tiron, Roxana. "Army Not Equipped to Manage Contractors on the Battlefield."

National Defense 88, no. 598 (September 2003): 32+.

Treverton, Gregory. *Reshaping National Intelligence in an Age of Information.* Cambridge, UK: Cambridge University Press, 2001.

_____. "Intelligence and the Market State." *Studies in Intelligence* 45, no. 10, Winter-Spring 2001, 69-76.

U.S. Army Central Command, Combined Arms Assessment Team (CAAT). "OPERATION ENDURING FREEDOM: CAAT Initial Impressions Report," September 2002. Ft. Leavenworth, KS: Center for Army Lessons Learned, 2002. URL: *<https://www.//call2.army.mil/products/iir/asp/BOSNIA/BHCAAT2/html/appc.asp>*. Accessed 3 September 2004.

U.S. Army Third Infantry Division. "OPERATION IRAQI FREEDOM Lessons Learned," May 2003. Ft. Leavenworth, KS: Center for Army Lessons Learned, 2003. URL: *<https: www.//call2.army.mil/products/on-point/asp/>*. Accessed 14 November 2004.

U.S. Army. Pamphlet 715-16 (Procurement), *Contractor Deployment Guide,* 27 February 1998. URL: *<http://www.army.mil/usapa/epubs/pdf/p715_16.pdf>*. Accessed 5 November 2004.

_____. Regulation 381-10, *U.S. Army Intelligence Activities,* Washington, DC: Department of the Army, July 1984.

_____. Field Manual (FM) 3-100. *Contractors on the Battlefield.* Washington, DC: Department of the Army, January 2003.

"U.S. Commercial Remote Sensing Policy Fact Sheet," *Office of Science and Technology Policy, Executive Office of the President,* 25 April 2003. URL: *<http://www.whitehouse.gov/news/releases/2003/05/20030513-8.html>*. Accessed 17 September 2004.

U.S. Congress, House. *IC21: Intelligence Community in the 21st Century,* 104th Cong., 1996. URL: *<http://www.gpoaccess.gov/int/int017.html>*, accessed 6 March 2006.

_____. *Intelligence Reform and Terrorism Prevention Act of 2004.* 108th Cong., 2d sess., 7 December 2004. URL: *<http://www.c-span.org/pdf/2004IntelAct.pdf>*. Accessed 7 March 2005.

_____. *Joint Inquiry into Intelligence Community Activities before and after the Terrorist Attacks of September 11, 2001.* 107th Cong., 2d sess., December 2002, URL: *<http://www.gpoaccess.gov/serialset/creports/911.html>*. Accessed 15 August 2004.

_____. *Permanent General Laws Relating to Indian Affairs, Revised Statues.* 44th Cong., 1st sess., 1876, Title XIV, Chapter 3, Sec. 1112 Indian Scouts. URL: *<http://digital.library.okstate.edu/kappler/Vol1/HTML_files/p1_22img.html>*. Accessed 29 October 2004.

_____. *Ronald W. Reagan National Defense Authorization Act for Fiscal Year 2005.* 108th Cong., 2nd sess., 20 January 2004. H.R. 4200. URL: *<http://www.wifcon.com/dodauth05.htm>*. Accessed 11 November 2004.

U.S. Congress, Senate. *Conference Committee Comments on Fiscal Year 2004 Intelligence Authorization Bill and Other Matters,* S. 108-044, 108th Cong.,

2nd sess., 8 May 2003. URL: <*http://www.fas.org/irp/congress/2003_rpt/ srpt108-44.html*>. Accessed 17 March 2005.

U.S. General Services Administration. *Federal Acquisition Regulation,* September 2001. URL: <*http://www.arnet.gov/far/*>. Accessed 6 October 2004.

U.S. Joint Forces Command. "Joint Lessons Learned: Operation IRAQI FREEDOM Major Combat Operations." Norfolk: Unpublished coordinating draft report dated 1 March 2004.

U.S. President, Executive Order 12333, "United States Intelligence Activities." 4 December 1981.

Verloy, Andre, and Daniel Politi. "Contracting Intelligence: Department of Interior Releases Abu Ghraib Contract." *The Center for Public Integrity* (28 July 2003). URL: <*http://www.publicintegrity.org/wow/report.aspx?aid=361&sid=100*>. Accessed 8 August 2004.

Voelz, Glenn, MAJ, USA. *Managing the Private Spies: The Use of Commercial Augmentation for Intelligence Operations.* MSSI Thesis, Washington, DC: Joint Military Intelligence College, 2005.

Wagner, Arthur L. *The Service of Security and Information.* Washington, DC: James L. Chapman, 1893.

Wayne, Lesie. "Pentagon Spends without Bids, a Study Finds," *New York Times,* online ed., 30 September 2004. URL: <*http://query.nytimes.com/gst/abstract.html?res= F00B14F93E5C0C738FDDA00894DC404482*>. Accessed 30 September 2004.

Weisman, Jonathan, and Thomas E. Ricks. "Increase in War Funding Sought: Bush Seeks Another $70 billion for Iraq and Afghanistan." *Washington Post,* online ed., 25 October 2004. URL: <*http://www.washingtonpost.com/ac2/wp-dyn/ A62554-2004Oct25?language=printer*>. Accessed 26 October 2004.

Younger, Raymond. *How Can the U.S. Army Effectively Outsource Tactical EW/SIGINT to Retain Mission Effectiveness?* MSSI Thesis, Washington, DC: Joint Military Intelligence College, 2002.

Witte, Griff. "Contractors were Poorly Monitored, GAO Says." *Washington Post,* online ed., 30 April 2005. URL: <*http://www.washingtonpost.com/wp-dyn/ content/article/2005/04/29/AR2005042901706.html*>. Accessed 11 May 2005.

www.ingramcontent.com/pod-product-compliance
Lightning Source LLC
Chambersburg PA
CBHW060204290526
45789CB00003B/1152